For Ce

Best Wishes,

Tim Holt

9.7.94

SONGS OF THE

SIMPLE LIFE

The Tim Holt Dam

And Other True Stories

Tim Holt

Suttertown Publishing
P.O. Box 214
Dunsmuir, California 96025

2nd Printing
ISBN No. 0-914485-20-2

Cover photo by Sandra Hood.

5/8/13   11 98

See last text page of this book for information about other
books from Suttertown Publishing.

For Sandra Hood,

who adorns our simple life

with her grace, her kindness,

and her generosity.

CONTENTS

SECTIONS

PREFACE: THE UNENCUMBERED LIFE

*A*merica, it seems to me, should be a country of singing and dancing, of fiddling and guitar playing, of hiking and exulting in our great stretches of countryside and wilderness. My America would have a central plaza in every city and town, and in the fine months there would be a public gathering there every weekend, with lots of food and music and dancing, all of it an implicit celebration of a practical, living democracy that brings disparate individuals and races together on common ground.

Unfortunately, the reality is that America has become a country of isolated individuals, isolated from each other and isolated from the land around us. We go from our climate-controlled offices, to our climate-controlled vehicles, to the climate-controlled mall, to our climate-controlled homes, where we sit in front of our computers and our televisions and our DVDs, and we might as well be living on the moon for all we know of the living world around us.

I am enough of a believer in the human spirit and human intelligence to know that this is not a lifestyle that most people would choose for themselves, any more than a wild animal would choose to live in a zoo. So I take it as a given that it is a lifestyle that we have been led into adopting, just as an animal might be enticed into a cage with a tempting morsel of food.

We have been tempted into the constricted lifestyle of the American consumer, and we are always running on the treadmill of getting and spending, wanting and buying. Our expectations of life are so limited, and we are so busy acquiring things, that we rarely connect with the life in ourselves or the life and the lives around us. It seems that we would rather tap out messages to strangers in cyberspace than sing out with our neighbors.

To live a simpler life inevitably involves raising expectations for our own lives—once we've shaken off the dust and debris of our present society—and to appreciate the value of listening to our own inner music. For there is self-interest as well as altruism in living The Simple Life, as one comes to recognize and reject the destructive aspects of our current society—destructive not only of the living world around us but of community life and the life within each of us.

Songs Of The Simple Life is a celebration of the joys and challenges of a life lived according to values very different from those of our present society. It is, indeed, a paean to simple pleasures, drawn from my own experiences on bike trips and in the mountains and in the world of print and in the small town where I live now. It is, in a sense, the saga of one person's escape from the narrow confines of American materialism and his ensuing exploration of a world of unencumbered living.

The articles and essays in this volume were written over the past quarter century. Some have already been published, some have been aired as commentaries on Jefferson Public Radio, and a few are being published here for the first time.

> Tim Holt
> Dunsmuir, California
> Summer 2001

A VERY SHORT BIOGRAPHY
OF THE AUTHOR'S LIFE

Many of the essays and articles in this collection are autobiographical. They are arranged by theme and are not in chronological order, so this brief sketch of the author's life may be helpful to the reader:

1948: Tim Holt born to Bill and Lodemia Holt in Sacramento, California. Grew up in quiet cul-de-sac in south part of town. Father was a civil engineer for the Western Pacific Railroad company.
1960: By age 12, author was already an avid reader. Read *Dr. Zhivago* this year, and got through the first 50 pages of *Das Kapital.* Couldn't make heads or tails of Marx's great work, but did learn new word: "intrinsic" (as in "the intrinsic value of labor").
1966-1971: Attended University of California at Berkeley during turbulent years of student protest. Author was somewhat apolitical in those days, however, and chose to begin journalism career by interviewing San Francisco's famous topless dancer, Carol Doda, for campus radio station. Got history degree in '71. With no solid career plans, took up writing after reading biography of Ernest Hemingway.
1971: Spent six weeks in Mexico, British Honduras (now Belize) and Guatemala. Saw first and only bullfight.
1971-1974: Freelance journalist and journalism student. Wrote mostly for publications in San Francisco Bay Area. Got degree in journalism in '73 from Columbia University.
Summer 1973: After getting journalism degree, spent six weeks in Europe, mostly France. This brief episode is referred to in "Confessions Of A Print Addict."
1975: Started newspaper, *The Suttertown News*, in hometown. For

3

19 years, until the enterprise ran out of money, this was a noble experiment in community journalism and voluntary poverty.

1995: Moved to Dunsmuir, California, the small town where his mother was raised, and where she and his father first met.

1995: Began publishing books, starting with *Old River Town,* a collection of reminiscences about Sacramento by writer and teacher Lloyd Bruno. This was followed by: *The Porch-Sitting Outlaw* (1998), a collection of Holt's non-fiction writing; *The Pilgrims' Chorus* (1999), Holt's young-adult novel about a dog who joins a wolf pack; and *On Higher Ground* (2000), his futuristic novel set in Northern California in the mid-21st century. He has been joined in this enterprise by life partner and Suttertown Publishing's art director, Sandra Hood.

INTRODUCTION: A CASE FOR
THE SIMPLE LIFE

Let not to get a living be thy trade, but thy sport.
—Henry Thoreau

In my own eyes I am a Hero Of The Road, a Poet Of the Open Road, an outcast from the mainstream of society, defiantly holding on to my hard-won sliver of roadway on the edge of traffic—as I pull my trailer loaded with sleeping bag, tent and cooking gear through the Northern California countryside to promote my books and reconnect with old friends.

Like Walt Whitman, I take what I please as I pass through the countryside, in the form of sights and smells and stories heard along the way. There is still something left of the pastoral life in this country, but you must seek it in odd, out-of-the-way places. What better way than on a bicycle, pedaling outside the mainstream of traffic?

One morning on a recent bike trip I loafed on the shores of Lake Merritt, in the teeming city of Oakland, and watched six little downy-feathered goslings feed in the clover-covered grass while their parents maintained a watchful vigilance.

In Anderson, near Redding, I learn of the coyote who lives in the farmer's field next to the little coffee shop where I stop for a break. The coyote has learned to follow the farmer's plow, feasting on the rodents that are turned up along with the earth. And he has mated with the big black she-dog that lives in the nearby neighborhood.

I camp one night in the Yuba Goldfields, where huge piles of rock tailings, the work of early-day gold dredgers, loom over pristine ponds scooped out by these same dredgers. The ponds teem with wildlife.

I learn from my travels that the wild is resilient, adaptable, taking advantage of a farmer's plow or an early-day gold dredger. The wild takes *our* tools, *our* labor, and adapts them to its own needs. The wilds operate with an intelligence that is honed and sharpened on the whetstone of survival.

It has taken me awhile—most of my life, really—to reach this simple appreciation of life and nature.

Like most of you, I was raised to be a good American consumer. One of my earliest memories is of wanting to wear plaid shirts because my father wore plaid shirts. When I was around six I wanted a pair of red low-topped tennis shoes because that was what the older boy next door wore. When I was 16 I badly wanted an XKE-Jaguar, similar to the car James Bond drove in those spy movies.

When I was young, in other words, I looked to material goods to define who I was—a *faux* identity conferred on me by possession and a certain amount of imagination. I put on a Superman cape and I became Superman. I put on a plaid shirt and I was a big, impressive grownup, like my father.

But even under a Superman cape, one assumes, there is a real person taking shape, a real identity slowly emerging. One of the perverse things about our present culture is that many adults never seem to get past the childhood notion that material possessions confer status and identity. Superman capes give way to big cars and big houses and the latest gadgets.

Why is it that we Americans never seem to get past this growing-up stage of life? Why are we in our supposedly mature years still trying to define who we are through material possessions? Don't we have identities and values of our own? If so, why do we need readymade status symbols? Are we as individuals and as a society in an arrested stage of development?

You would think that as people mature they would increasingly resist the pressure of our modern consumer culture. As adults, *we* should be telling the society what we want to buy, not the other way around. I know that I am better able than I was at 13 or 16 or even 24 to make my own purchasing decisions because I am much more aware of who I am. I didn't really develop my current passion for bicycling, for example, until I had started my fourth decade, but I have not owned a car for the past 20 years. Although I was a complete TV addict as a kid, I have never owned one and nowadays spend most of my evenings reading. And there are times when I am in complete rebellion against the consumer culture, actually patching and mending things rather than throwing them away.

For me, reaching the early stages of adulthood meant not only developing my own identity but at the same time nurturing a sense of independence, a freedom from *wanting.* I am no longer willing to allow our modern consumer culture to run roughshod over my life, to tell me what objects I must purchase. In a positive sense, this means avoiding the din of commercials, forgoing the distractions of material possession, and instead building a life that reflects my own values and interests.

I would, if I could, borrow the muse of Walt Whitman for this book, for I too aim to write a paean to the human spirit and to the majesty of human sweat and human labor. Alas, I am not Walt Whitman, and this book is only a paltry, flickering candle in a dark age, but at least it is something.

Why do I call this a "dark age"? Our present society portrays humanity in many, many different ways as weak and spiritless and increasingly unable to function in the world without all sorts of aids, as if we were all living in some vast, beneficent nursing home. Citizens who would rebel if told how to vote or what religion to practice, docilely march out to the mall in lockstep and purchase the latest computer software. Children, it seems, cannot play without the aid of the latest video games. How have we allowed ourselves to be told what to buy and when to buy it, to be bound into a kind of economic fascism?

We dance to the corporate tune, and this has drowned out our inner music. After decades of advertising, our "needs" are no longer inner-driven or community-driven but corporate-driven. There is certainly no innate human need for a particular item of computer software or a video game. At most, these are pleasant luxuries. But they are the lifeblood of the modern corporation. They keep the assembly lines humming and the profits flowing. Imagine the chaos and devastation that would ensue if we all looked at our pile of possessions and said, "That's enough!"

But that cannot be allowed to happen. A case must be made for each new item, and the frantic hype is in direct proportion to the superfluity of the object. It takes a great deal of energy to create a need where there is none, after all. Thus we have the intensity with which the latest digital camera or high-resolution television is hyped. We are told in breathless phrases that this latest product is going to make a quantum improvement in our lives. What's hard to understand is why any sane person would take this corporate hype seriously, or see it as anything other than the propaganda of desperate, needy corporations in their mindless quest for profits.

But we have come to see things from the corporate viewpoint. Only 40 years ago consumers scoffed at the ludicrous assertion that a dishwashing detergent could be "new" or "revolutionary." But in computers and other techno-gadgets the corporate world has found the right sort of trinkets to dangle in front of the skeptical consumer. What fire and gunpowder were to natives, so computers and their accouterments are to modern man—a form of magic whose workings we do not understand and are therefore clothed in a God-like power and mystique that we have been led to believe can truly change our lives for the better—"revolutionize" them, if you will.

We have come to accept the idea that if we purchase the latest gadget, a digital camera or a high-resolution TV, that our lives are on the right track, that we are part of some vaguely defined thing called "progress." All we can be certain of is that this "progress" is of a very limited scope, bounded by narrow-minded, commercially driven parameters. For we have come to measure all human endeavor in terms of goods and money and profits.

We ask not what was the best movie of the last season, but what was the *top-grossing* movie. And whether that shortstop is really worth $10 million a year. And if Citizen X can run for public office with less than $2 million in her campaign chest. A racecar driver dies in a crash at Daytona and the headline reads: "He Earned $41 Million During Career." Junior won't help with the chores unless he receives his weekly stipend. Sis's reward for good grades is a crisp five-dollar bill. Skip the funeral; we just want to know what's in the will.

Have you heard? You can now buy all the goods you want at rock-bottom prices via the Internet. By the standards of today this becomes a milestone along the path of human progress.

Behold the modern multinational corporations, who bestride the Earth like Great Colossuses, knowing no national boundaries, doing their business wherever labor and natural resources can be bought at the lowest price.

There are many in this country who bemoan the fate of the employees of these great corporations—those poor, exploited workers in the fields and sweatshops overseas. But do we have to look abroad to find an exploited class? Look around you. Look in the mirror, for that matter. Haven't most of us been reduced, like our brethren overseas, to a cramped, peasant-like existence? Brainwashed, cajoled, and prodded to want the latest, the newest, the most improved, we are typically chained down to jobs with no more meaning than the next paycheck, in order to chip away at a mountain of credit card debt. It seems that most of us are trapped in a kind of economic slavery, chained down to jobs whether we like them or not, just so we can keep buying stuff.

And for all this soul-deadening work and sacrifice, our reward is the regular trip to the shopping mall, where we accept the latest trinkets and toys as if these were fair compensation for the freedom that has been sacrificed. American freedom, as we know it today, 212 years after the adoption of the Bill of Rights, is most frequently practiced in the aisle of a Wal-Mart (or more recently on the Internet), where we have the freedom to choose between the green one or the red one, the blue or the yellow.

Our obsession with consuming the latest and the newest products has turned us into a passive society. We modern consumers lead a very limited existence, going from home to car to office to car to shopping mall to car and back home, rarely making or growing anything for ourselves, rarely getting out in the open and walking from one place to another. Just as the ever-toiling, subservient peasant of the Middle Ages was essential to the existence of the nobility, so our modern, obeisant consumer, content with his or her carefully defined and circumscribed patch of existence, enables the modern corporation to exist and flourish.

God forbid that we should get out of our cars and take a walk in the woods. It might start a revolution!

But, instead, here we are, cut off from the rest of the living world in our cars, our climate-controlled houses and offices and shopping malls—and when you are this disconnected it is inevitable that you are going to treat the natural world as a kind of all-you-can-consume buffet.

The average North American consumes five times as much of the world's resources as the average African, and three times as much as the average Asian. And, as we're beginning to see, our consumption-oriented lifestyle is beginning to have serious consequences not only for ourselves but for the rest of the planet as well. On the one hand, we're shackled to often meaningless jobs to keep up those car payments and buy the latest gadgets. And this same obsession with consumption has prompted the slow unraveling and destruction of our living world.

In 1998 a first-ever worldwide inventory of the world's natural resources by the World Conservation Monitoring Center of Cambridge, England and two other agencies found that since 1960:

—Human use of freshwater resources had doubled to the point where humans were using half of all available supplies, threatening the world's remaining wetlands and the species who depend on them.

—Global consumption of wood and paper had increased by two-thirds, with most of the world's forests being cut at an unsustainable rate.

—Marine fish consumption had more than doubled, with most of the world's fish species either fully exploited or in decline.

—Emissions of carbon dioxide, the primary greenhouse gas, had doubled, which has prompted estimates of an increase of as much as 11 degrees fahrenheit in average worldwide warming by the end of this century.

A study published in 2002 by the National Academy of Sciences estimates that current worldwide use of resources—in farming, fishing, mining, and construction—is over-consuming the Earth's resources at a rate of 120 percent; in other words, 20 percent more than the Earth is able to generate each year.

It's the credit card mentality applied to the Earth's resources. It is a path leading to resource bankruptcy.

Nature has not given our 300-year-old industrial/technological society a license to exploit as it pleases; indeed, there are serious signs that we are reaching the limits of exploitation. Nature is beginning to say what we have for so long been unwilling to say: "Enough!" The polar caps are melting—vast chunks, some the size of the state of Delaware, are breaking off the Antarctic cap. In the

Arctic, ships are finding open water where they once had to break through seas of ice.

In equatorial Africa, the ice cap of Mount Kilimanjaro, it is predicted, will disappear in another 15 years. Already, the glaciers are disappearing from Glacier National Park in Montana. University of California scientists predict that the snowpack in the Sierras will diminish by as much as 82 percent by the end of this century, having serious implications for both agricultural and municipal supplies of water.

And if we continue to live our narrow, self-absorbed existence, we may yet experience, within the next half century, deadly heat waves, raging forest fires and the resulting pollution, and a disappearing coastline as ocean levels rise. If we do not choose to connect with the earth, it will connect with us—and with a vengeance.

Two opposing ideas are gradually emerging in response to all this. One is the so-called Space Station mentality, or what I call the Bubble Lifestyle, in which we increasingly retreat to our climate-controlled cars, our climate-controlled homes and our climate-controlled offices. As the climate grows hotter and hotter, the air more stifling, more filled with ozone and the fires from tinderbox conditions in our surrounding forests, aren't we more and more likely to drift into this Space Station existence?

But there *is* an escape from this fate. It begins with planting a garden, baking one's own bread, going for a walk in the woods rather than the mall—in other words, learning to live simply and be resourceful rather than simply using resources. It is a humbler attitude than we have taken up until now in this country. It will ultimately mean, as Ernest Callenbach expressed it in *Ecotopia,* taking our "modest place in a seamless . . . web of living organisms, disturbing that web as little as possible."

One can glean a few signs of change here and there: In Southern California concern over the environment has gotten to the point where sheriffs deputies are patrolling coastal tidepools to protect small sea life forms from poachers. In Northern California, on a stretch of freeway between Truckee and Reno, the first-ever "mammal undercrossings" are being installed under the freeway to save the lives of deer, bears and other animals. Germany has recently included protections for animals in its constitution. And in the last few years there has been a proliferation of no-kill animal shelters in the U.S.

These are scattered but hopeful signs that the long isolation of the human species from other life forms may yet come to an end.

* * *

Henry Thoreau has a lovely passage at the end of *Walden*. He recounts the story, going the rounds of New England, of a "strong and beautiful bug" hatched out of an old table that had sat in a farmer's kitchen for 60 years. Perhaps hatched by the heat of an urn, it was heard gnawing its way through the table for several weeks.

"Who does not feel his faith in a resurrection and immortality strengthened by hearing of this?" he asks. "Who knows what beautiful and winged life, whose egg has been buried for ages under many concentric layers of woodenness in the dead dry life of society . . . may unexpectedly come forth from amidst society's most trivial and handselled furniture, to enjoy its perfect summer life at last!"

In our own age, what will it take, I wonder, to set each of us gnawing out of our own self-made traps? And what will we find when we emerge from under our piles of debris and gadgetry? If we were to sweep away the mental cobwebs, the tedious concerns of our consumer society, what paths might open before us?

It is, at least, an experiment worth trying.

TOWARD

A

SIMPLER LIFE

HENRY'S DAY

*T*his country has unofficial holidays devoted to *not* smoking and *not* watching TV. What we need now is a day set aside for not *buying* stuff, a chance for every American consumer to sample, however briefly, The Simple Life.

Our overflowing landfills need a respite. A nation awash in credit card debt needs an excuse, just like its smokers, to break a debilitating habit.

Throughout the year we're told to buy, buy buy. Surely we can set aside one day for a saner message: "Shall we always study to obtain more of these things, and not sometimes to be content with less? . . . [We] are employed . . . laying up treasures which moth and rust will corrupt and thieves break through and steal. It is a fool's life . . ."

So wrote the nation's most celebrated Non-Consumer, Henry David Thoreau, in *Walden*. What better date than July 12, Thoreau's birthday, for this holiday from consumerism? Who better to represent The Simple Life than this high-principled curmudgeon who blew the first warning trumpet at the dawn of the Age of Consumption?

He built his own 10-by-15-foot cabin at Walden Pond for $28 in materials and grew his own food there. His furniture consisted of a table, a chair and a bed. For a short time there were three ornamental pieces of limestone rock on the table, but Thoreau soon decided these were superfluous, throwing them out when he found he had to dust them every day.

Henry Thoreau

We really should start our holiday on July 4th and cap it off eight days later with a birthday party for Mr. Thoreau (no presents, please). Imagine people publicly shredding their credit cards, smashing their TVs, their DVDs, their (*quel sacrilege!*) computers—now that would be a *real* Independence Day.

For our poster boy, it would be hard to improve on Thoreau's image of the farmer of his day: "How many a poor immortal soul have I met well nigh crushed and smothered under its load, creeping down the road of life, pushing before it a barn 75 feet by 40, its Augean stables never cleansed, and one hundred acres of land, tillage, mowing, pasture, and wood-lot!"

Thoreau was one of the country's first advocates and practitioners of voluntary poverty. He found that The Simple Life left him with plenty of time to pursue his real interests. He did have a number of practical skills—including land-surveying, carpentry, and tree-pruning—which he put to use when he needed cash. But the bulk of his time was spent on what we would think of as leisure pursuits: writing in his journal, exploring the countryside around Concord, sometimes just sitting for long periods of time and staring at a lake, a tree, or a woodchuck. But he wasn't just fooling around. Thoreau was an avid naturalist who also sought answers to the deepest spiritual questions in the natural world.

Walden was published in 1854, when an economy based on mass consumption by city dwellers was just beginning to supplant the more self-sufficient, rural economy. Thoreau held up a cautionary hand to his fellow citizens and argued, quite reasonably, that the time they spent working to buy more and more things could be spent more profitably: "Most of the luxuries, and many of the so-called comforts of life, are not only not indispensable, but positive hindrances to the elevation of mankind," he wrote in *Walden*. The more things you owned, the more time you had to spend dusting (and nowadays adjusting, installing, downloading, upgrading, and replacing), whereas a ramble in the woods would nurture body, mind and soul.

Having read the foregoing, you probably won't be surprised to learn that I've never owned a TV and sold my last car 18 years ago. And, yes, I spend a lot of my time writing and rambling in the woods near my home. I suspect that there are more of us in this country practicing Thoreau's creed, or at least trying to, than the media lets on. You do occasionally see a Simple Life story elbowing its way through the usual media mix of sex and political scandal and crime.

A holiday recognizing one of this nation's more original thinkers would be a welcome sign that we're starting to look beyond the shallow consumerism of the past century and a half.

The health of the Gross National Product, the very existence of the modern commercial world as we know it, depends on the lockstep conformity of masses of consumers opening their wallets and purses in obeisance to the manipulations of mass marketing. If you can free yourself from this advertising-induced regimentation, you've taken the first step toward the freedom that Thoreau contemplated when he wrote this passage in *Walden*: "If a man does not keep pace with his companions, perhaps it is because he hears a different drummer. Let him step to the music he hears, however measured or far away."

So tune out the advertising jingles on July 12th, take some inspiration from Henry Thoreau, and let your own music come through loud and clear. It might be sweeter than you ever thought possible.

AMERICANS & GADGETS

*N*o doubt about it, Americans have what amounts to an obsession with gadgetry.

There was the recent photo in the *New York Times*, which showed a row of college students with laptops, responding via e-mail to their professor, who was right there in the room.

This obsessive use of the latest gadgets doesn't make much sense, unless, that is, you apply the Logic of Gadgetry, which is that when a gadget exists, you use it whenever possible. So you drive your car rather than walk two blocks. You buy your books on the Internet rather than from the neighborhood bookstore.

Now, having access to the latest gadgetry does have its advantages; I myself have occasionally found cell phones, the Internet, e-mail and all that helpful. But I like to keep them at arm's length. It is one thing to use them as tools at work, quite another to bring them home, with all their intrusions and disruptions.

And, please, spare me all the high-fallutin' stuff about the "educational benefits" of the Internet and the wonderful connections you can make with e-mail. Growing up in the fifties, I was in the earliest TV generation. This was when, just like the Internet now, TV was being hyped as a potentially wonderful educational medium. With live drama on programs like "Playhouse 90," television in those days actually did have some promise of enriching the home environment, much as a good library does. Those programs are still there, of course, on PBS and some of the cable stations, but in practice television has proven to be a great medium for making a few people very rich, while the masses are provided with mind-numbing amusement.

But of course, the Internet will be different.

As we now know, television has proven to be one of the truly destructive forces in American life. Television is the gabby relative who came to visit 50 years ago and never left. There it sits in the corner, even now, babbling its inanities, never shutting up, demanding the attention that Mom and Dad and the kids ought to be lavishing on each other.

Don't we already have enough intrusions on the American family? Does it make sense to introduce yet another intruder into the American home, so that when family members aren't being pulled from each other by television or the DVD, they go to the Internet? Can it be very far into the future when each family member will have his or her own home entertainment module, complete with TV, DVD, computer and VRH (Virtual Reality Headset)?

Is that where we want to go as a society? To become more and more isolated from each other in our electronic wombs? Are we so distracted by these gadgets that we've lost the ability to see where all this is headed?

In that regard all I can say is, thank God for the French. According to a report on National Public Radio, 42 percent of those surveyed in France don't have personal computers and don't intend to buy one. The reasons they gave were that computers are too expensive, too complicated, and "too corrosive to personal relations."

What a wonderful example of independent thinking that is, amid all the current hype about dot-coms and web sites. What a refreshing notion that, as a thinking person, you can actually pick and choose among high-tech gadgets, discarding those that may actually be "corrosive" to your personal life.

While I have found some of the latest high-tech gadgets useful in my working life, in my home life I really don't need to be bombarded with more information or more messages needing an immediate response. What I need are more of the true luxuries of modern life: the time to reflect, to relax, to do absolutely nothing. Why are most of us, in our tap-tap-tapping and our click-click-clicking, frantically running away from those very things?

OUR SHRINKING PUBLIC SPACES

*P*eople chattering away in movie houses, talking loudly over cell phones in restaurants—what we're seeing increasingly nowadays is what I call the "privatization of public spaces." Those folks who chatter away at the movies are carving out a little chat room, a mini-living room, if you will, to the detriment of the group experience.

This chipping away at public spaces, piece by piece, is graphically evident on my daily morning walk to the post office. I seem to recall from my youthful days that there was a time when a public sidewalk was generally recognized as a space for pedestrians. Nowadays it's a rare morning when I don't encounter cars parked across the sidewalk. Usually these have been placed there by people who haven't bothered to pull forward the few extra feet into their driveway so pedestrians can pass by without walking in the gutter.

Now, I doubt that the chatterboxes in the movie theatres *intend* to spoil the picture for those around them any more than those thoughtless motorists *intend* to block my path. I think in most cases it's just that they are functioning in a kind of personal bubble.

We're dealing with a deep-seated problem here, one that will probably not be helped by yet another plea for more politeness or consideration for others.

Let's face it: The American lifestyle has become increasingly compartmentalized and privatized as we've become a more affluent society.

In an earlier era, more people rode buses and trolleys to work or school because not as many people owned cars. Now Dad and Mom are likely drive to work every day as single passengers in separate vehicles. Junior and Sis, by the time they get to high school, may be commuting there in their own cars, too.

Back in that more communal era, the same people who were riding buses and trolleys were flocking in droves to the movie houses—no TV or videos in those days.

Today we are un-learning the communal experience of that previous generation. Much more of our time nowadays is spent in isolation—in the car, in front of the TV, DVD, or computer. It's hardly surprising that we find it more and more difficult to get out of our little bubbles when we enter what remains of our public spaces.

My concern is that this phenomenon is likely to feed on itself. As the chattering continues in the movie theatres, more and more people will opt to watch videos at home, thus further diminishing the communal experience. Put enough barriers in the way of pedestrians, and we'll all be in single-passenger vehicles, cruising down the street in our self-contained bubbles.

And yet, thank God, there is still something left at the grassroots core of our social fabric: things like block parties, farmers markets, street festivals. These are like fine old quilts: a little dusty and musty in this modern era, but finely woven together, often out of very diverse elements. They are held right at street level, where everyone can participate, and for just this reason they teach, for all their quaint folksiness, one of the basic lessons of a civilized society. They are places where people of all ages and races and incomes can still learn a vanishing art: that of sharing public spaces in a manner considerate of others.

WHY I'M NOT THE UNABOMBER

*F*irst of all, I don't have a degree from Harvard, I bathe regularly, have never taught math at UC Berkeley, I did not make bombs as a kid, nor have I had the remotest desire to blow up complete strangers.

Having gotten all that out of the way, hopefully it's safe to admit that I make my own bread, bring my own bag to the market, visit the local library a lot, do not own a car or a TV, and bike or walk pretty much everywhere I go.

In the wake of all those revelations about Ted Kaczynski, I think it's important to make this clear: You can live lightly on the Earth without wanting to blow up or otherwise injure those you may feel are wrecking it.

You see, I appreciate Mr. Kaczynski's principled and intelligent opposition to our current obsession with technology, and I admire his back-to-basics lifestyle, but I'm concerned that his other habits may be giving The Simple Life a bad name.

I'm not just referring to his violent tendencies here; I'm also referring to his social isolation. I live a fairly simple life, materially and technologically, because I believe it is healthier for myself and the planet. But I also have simplified my life so I can spend more of

This essay was first published in 1996.

31

my waking hours on activities other than earning money to buy adult toys. These activities include reading, hiking and biking in the mountainous area where I live (not Montana), and being involved in a small town's community activities.

Even that famous so-called recluse, Henry David Thoreau, who also built his own cabin in the woods and made his own bread, was by no means a complete hermit. He certainly spent a lot of his Simple-Life generated time alone, communing with nature. But he also used some of it to party, after his own fashion, with his transcendentalist friends in that cabin.

In its best sense, The Simple Life is defined not by what it avoids (technological obsession and rampant consumerism) but by what it seeks: meaningful endeavors and better relations with other people. This can mean something as obvious as spending more time in family activities and less time in front of the TV. In my case it means writing, gardening, and participating in the local farmers' market. It means that I do not spend any time fiddling with the latest computer programs, cruising the lake on my jet skis, or watching "Oprah." To the extent that I can avoid these distractions, I am more likely to make choices for my life that are in fact *my* choices—not those thrust on me by someone's need to make a corporate buck.

I agree with Mr. Kaczynski that much of modern technology and its accompanying commercialism is anti-human, alienating, and destructive to the natural world. But I fail to see how using technology to kill or seriously injure one's fellow human beings offers a real alternative. To a large extent, that approach mimics the worst practices of our current society.

CONNECTING

THE OPEN ROAD

Afoot and light-hearted I take to the open road,
Healthy, free, the world before me,
The long brown path before me, leading wherever I choose.
> *Walt Whitman's"Poem Of The Open Road,"*
> *from* Leaves Of Grass

My introduction to the pleasures of bicycling came in the middle of my struggles as a small-time newspaper publisher.

For 19 years I published a small, underfunded weekly newspaper in Sacramento. I wrote most of the paper's cover stories and countless of its news and feature stories. There were also ads to be sold, tax forms to be filled out, the constant need to interview and hire people due to the low wages and high turnover, and all the other dreary minutiae that go with being the chief factotum in a small business.

It seemed we were always running to catch up, whether it was to meet a yawning deficit in our bank balance or one of the ever-present deadlines.

The job of editor/publisher of this small paper, as exalted as it was in some respects, also locked me in a kind of self-imposed prison, with an indefinite sentence. There seemed little chance of even a brief escape beyond the one week a year, at Christmas, when we didn't publish a paper.

About five years into this madness I sold my car, a Volkswagen bug, to pay off some of the paper's debts. For awhile I got around on a moped, but finally abandoned motorized transport entirely. To get around town, I purchased a durable Raleigh three-speed with a wide, comfortable seat and a sturdy frame. I had never thought of this sturdy clunker as anything other than a city bike—until one Sunday, when, feeling energetic, I pointed it south down the road that runs along the Sacramento River. I must have had a tail wind that morning, because my memory is of *skimming* down that road almost effortlessly, even on that heavy bike. By midday I found myself, miraculously, in the little Delta town of Walnut Grove, 30 miles down the river road from Sacramento. That day I had taken the first major step out of my self-imposed prison.

From then on it was a matter of pushing the boundaries out a little farther with each trip. I took a quantum leap in this direction when an inheritance from a great aunt enabled me to buy a fancy new racing bike. It weighed about half as much as my clunker, and I was now able to push farther into the Delta, or to head east into the rolling hills of the Capay Valley, and to make forays into the Sierra Nevada foothills.

So now I had a simple antidote when the pressures of the job became too intense. I strapped on my backpack, hopped on my bike, and hit the road. There was always a feeling of delicious freedom when I passed the city's limits. The mind cleared, burdens were left behind in the busy city; there was only the road passing under my wheels, the wind in my face, and two or three days of leisure ahead. On a bicycle there is nothing to cut you off from the river, the road, the wind, the sun's heat, the rustling leaves, the smells—no wind-

shield to limit your view, no radio or tape player to block the sounds. On a hot summer day when you're out on the Open Road there can come a time—usually when you've covered a lot of miles and you're too tired to think, when the road, the river, the trees, the sky—and you—all melt into one shimmering whole.

One of the many sins of the automobile is that it causes us to miss a great deal. The car enables us to go farther, and, paradoxically, see less.

On my bicycle, I have time to savor the sights along the way. I am always traveling back roads; the quiet of the countryside is disturbed only by the barely audible whir of my tires on the road. This quiet mode of travel has let me catch glimpses of shy animals like coyotes and wild turkeys.

Indeed, encountering the unexpected is one of the delights of this mode of travel. Had I been whizzing along at 50 or 60 miles an hour, would I have noticed that strange collection of empty bottles arranged in geometrical patterns on someone's front lawn? Or seen that blue heron taking off?

One winter I worked in a bookstore ten miles from my home. My bicycle commute to work was in mountain country. In the dead of winter, the trip over snow-covered roads could take two hours, while the same trip in an auto on the freeway took 20 minutes. But anyone who's ever felt the soft pelting of snowflakes on their face or been surrounded by a fairyland of snow-dusted trees knows which route and which mode of travel was the more rewarding. Bicycling is a prime example of how taking more time to do something actually adds to one's quality of life.

In an age of faxes, e-mail, and store-bought bread, bicycling is in another world—one of handwritten letters, long, meandering conversations, and the smell of fresh-baked bread. The quiet, steady whir of those wheels on the road keeps saying: Enjoy the journey.

RYER ISLAND AND THE RIVER PEOPLE

*O*ff the main river road south of Sacramento there is an enchanting region of islands separated by sloughs. The islands and the sloughs are the artificial creations of ambitious 19th century farmers, who by means of a system of levees that created the islands, uncovered the rich bottom land of the Sacramento River's floodplain. It is a sparsely populated region of farms, a few ferries, and marinas located in some of the wider stretches of the sloughs.

My bicycle rides in these remote stretches of the Sacramento River Delta were on the levee roads that skirted the sloughs and ran around the perimeters of the islands. Occasionally I would see people fishing in the sloughs down below, or, on the island side, farmers working in their fields, but for the most part I passed through an unpopulated landscape.

My favorite of the Delta islands is Ryer. It is about 20 miles in circumference, and, at the time of this writing, boasts two ferries. One connects it to a point on the mainland close to the town of Rio Vista, and the other to Grand Island on its eastern side. The island's other link to the rest of the world is a bridge at its northern end.

There are marinas at three locations around the island, but despite this, and its three links with the outside world, Ryer Island

This article was written in 1994 and first published in 1998.

41

always seemed to me to be a quiet, tranquil world unto itself. Relatively little traffic passes along the levee road, or the island's only other road, one that runs east and west and cuts the island in two.

After my first few trips to Ryer Island, I learned to look for its landmarks. I couldn't miss the big silo-like structures looming up over the fields to the south as soon as I entered the island. (Even though there were several large buildings in this complex, I don't ever recall seeing a human being anywhere near them.) Directly across the slough from the complex were some old farm buildings, crumbling wooden structures in an advanced state of decay. Farther on toward Rio Vista I would see the same sizeable boat-under-construction in a makeshift drydock, always, it seemed, in the same stage of partial completion. After that the slough widened dramatically into a lush marshland, where ducks and the occasional fishing boats left their watery trails.

Soon after this the levee road skirts along a deep water channel, the region's own Erie Canal, linking San Francisco Bay to the Port of Sacramento. Here, of course, the boat traffic greatly increases, both in numbers and size of vessels, and there are generally more people fishing on these banks than anywhere else on the island. Here it is that you can get your first view of the two large bridge towers looming up from the river at its widest point at Rio Vista.

It is on the land side of this stretch of Ryer Island that I have seen vineyards growing alongside cornfields, an unexpected merging of the Midwest and the Mediterranean. I have heard stories of a rail line that ran all the way around the island at one time, moving heavy loads of produce to markets outside. Here on this side are suggestions that the island has, or had, links to a wider world, and it is from this side that the Ryer Island Ferry shuttles back and forth between the island and the mainland near the town of Rio Vista.

I sensed that there were mysteries on the island that, as a tourist on a bicycle, were well beyond my grasp. What possible mysteries? After all, Ryer Island is not a region of shadows. Or murky swamps and dense vegetation. It is open farm country for the most part, painted more in shades of green than in gloomy, mysterious colors. But it *is* a quiet country, and its open spaces allow the traveler room for his or her imagination to roam.

A friend took an extended houseboat tour of the Delta's sloughs and told me of seeing, on top of one levee, a complete sound system set up, with amplifiers and the whole works, but with nary a soul in sight. Anyone who has spent much time in the Sacramento Delta will find that story credible.

Not all my time in the Delta was spent cycling on lonely roads. In my travels from one little town to another, I rubbed shoulders with a number of the river country's residents. Some I met in the natural course of my travels. One of these was Steamboat Slough Ferry captain Mike Deusenberry. Others, like Captain Jim Clove, were off the beaten track. Many of them, like Deusenberry and Clove, became the focus for stories in my weekly newspaper, *The Suttertown News*.

Deusenberry's job as captain and crew of the Steamboat Slough Ferry was to transport cars, their passengers and the occasional cyclist between Ryer and Grand islands. His ferry moved along a heavy cable strung between the islands. So there was no steering required, and Deusenberry's job was pretty much limited to regulating the ferry's speed. From his post in the ferry's operating tower, Deusenberry viewed the same stretch of river hour after hour, day after day.

Deusenberry was, in fact, an employee of the state's massive transportation agency, CalTrans, which operated his ferry and the one on the Rio Vista side of the island toll-free. Deusenberry was in a remote, unsupervised backwater of the state agency, and he took full advantage of his position. Not a timid or quiet man, the full-bearded, well-fed young captain was in a state of open rebellion against the routine and boring aspects of his job—which, on a self-guided ferry making 60 round trips a day, could be mind-numbing. (When a bicyclist missed the ferry one day and was left waiting at the dock, Deusenberry muttered, as much to himself as to anyone else, "Don't worry, I'll come back. I *always* come back.")

The message stenciled across the front of Deusenberry's hard hat read: "Y. B. NORMAL." He lived that motto with gusto. As he chugged along—back and forth, back and forth, in a seemingly endless routine—he made full use of what he called his "si-reeen." The siren's loud wail was supposed to warn boaters of danger from the ferry's submerged cable, but more often during the times I was on board it served as accompaniment to Deusenberry's frequent whooping and hollering. When the "si-reeen" and Deusenberry were both at full volume, they were sometimes joined by a rooster on a Grand Island farm in an unholy trio of voices that was enough to raise the dead and send them right back where they came from.

Another "captain," a much quieter and more reclusive one, also lived in the river country. I encountered him one day on a bike trip along the river just past West Sacramento. I spied an older man

Captain Jim Clove with shipmate.

wearing a seafaring hat, walking in the distance with about half a dozen dogs and two goats.

He called himself "Captain" Jim Clove, and he lived on a replica of a 16th century Spanish galleon he'd built himself. Although probably well into his 60s, Clove had the trim, wiry build of someone who'd been physically active all his life. His ship was moored on the river directly across from a collection of restaurants and a marina. Not really an unsociable man, Captain Jim occasionally rowed across and joined the crowd at one of the restaurant's bars. Most of his time, however, was spent on his ship or roaming up and down his side of the river. When I met him, he was sharing the ship with his six dogs, two goats, a rabbit, about 60 pigeons, and a sparrow hawk with a broken wing.

Captain Jim was a soft-spoken, very gentle man, a soft touch for injured or stray animals. There was a hint of sadness about him, due, I surmised, to a young woman who had sailed with him to Sacramento 15 years ago but had since departed.

So he had surrounded himself with companions of another sort. Every spring and summer he had regular visits from a Canadian goose who would swim near the ship, keeping a wary eye on the dogs. He doted on the injured hawk, who shared his living quarters below deck; to nurse it back to health, he lovingly fed it raw chicken parts. He told with sadness of the poor diseased rabbit he'd found in a tattered cardboard box along the river, apparently placed there and left to die by its owner. This one was past saving; he'd had to shoot it.

The dogs and goats were confined to the ship's topside, but the birds and the rabbit had the run of the living quarters below deck; the residue of pigeon droppings he tolerated down there was another measure of his love for animals.

But Sacramento's growth was closing in on his snug little outpost. Traffic on the river was increasing, the marina on the other side of the river was expanding, and there were plans in the works for a golf course, restaurants and condominiums on the riverbank where the captain was moored. When I published a piece about him in April 1987, he'd been told he had six months to clear out. Soon after that he was gone. The vegetation along that part of the river would soon be mowed down, including the wild grapes and berries that the captain had harvested for himself and his shipmates. The trails he had wandered with his menagerie would be paved over.

Once again, Sacramento no doubt thought it was making "progress." As for the captain, there were plenty of other moorings off the beaten track; he would just have to stay one step ahead of the bulldozer.

It would be an understatement to say that Gloria Crissinger ran her little Delta restaurant with a personal touch. For one thing, there was her doll collection scattered about the small dining room, in every nook or corner where a little plastic cherub could fit. She even made special pancakes shaped like dolls for kids to eat. The jukebox was filled with her favorite tunes, from swing music to cowboy songs, and she was always happy to sit down at your table and talk about her childhood in Chicago, where her father made part of his living renting sound trucks to politicians.

As one of the three business establishments in the town of Clarksburg, Gloria's Hof Brau was an easy find on one of my first bike trips through the Delta. The food was never better than mediocre, although I can remember devouring a turkey dinner there with relish after a bike trip of 60 miles.

Well into her 60s when I met her, Gloria had run a string of bars and restaurant-bars in the Bay Area before she and her husband Frank had opted for a quieter life along the river. She was the quintessential innkeeper, a little weary and doughy-faced from all those late hours, but still able to fill the small establishment with her personal warmth—and charm a city-weary newspaperman with rambling discussions of her philosophy of life, which was well thought out. She was people-smart and a practiced expert at massaging her customers' egos. Hers was a nimble personality. There was a bar adjacent to the dining area with about five or six stools, and she retained the barroom habit of calling her male customers "honey," "sweetheart," or "doll-baby." One minute she was a saloon queen, warming lonely hearts and trading jokes and gossip with the men on the barstools; the next she was a salon queen, entertaining a "literary" man from the big city.

Gloria's Hof Brau wasn't really a business; it was more an exercise in self-expression. The open river country and the remoteness of their outposts had given her and Mike Deusenberry and Captain Jim the opportunity to exercise a kind of creative license with their lives. I don't think any of them could have done what they were doing in the city. Certainly not Deusenberry nor Captain Jim. And Gloria, with minimal overhead and little competition, had the luxury of just being herself—folksy, warm, motherly, lovably corny.

Gloria Crissinger and Captain Jim and Mike Deusenberry provided glimpses of what one's life could be like outside the confines of the city. Growing increasingly restless there within the rigid demands of a weekly newspaper, I began to feel that it was time for more than a temporary escape.

REVELATIONS

This is an excerpt from my novel, On Higher Ground, *set in the mid-21st century against a narrative backdrop of advanced global warming, rampant pollution, and cities covered by climate-controlling domes. In this episode, two refugees from the San Francisco Bay Area are exploring the Mount Shasta region, where they are dazzled by a rare encounter with the natural world.*

The next day was one of exploring. Early that morning, Jess and Susan hopped in the truck with Tim, who was taking a load of produce down to Redding. They got out of the truck just south of Dunsmuir, and, following Tim's directions, walked a short way along a paved road until they got to a dirt road, likely an old logging road, that led to the north side of the rugged Castle Crags.

The path was mostly in shade at the start, winding through a forest of incense cedars and pine. The novelty of being surrounded by tall trees, of breathing the crisp morning air filled with the muted scents of timber and pine needles, served to lift their spirits and push them along the path with seemingly little effort.

A creek ran roughly parallel to the road they were following. On the other side of the creek were the massive crags. There was still snow on their crests. The water from melting snow in the upper reaches of the crags had over the eons carved smooth streambeds out of the rough granite, and these creased the steep slopes all along their rough facade. Along each steep watercourse there were frequent waterfalls, and these had scooped out little green pools at their bases, so that each slender stream of water was laced with shimmering aqua-green beads from one end to the other.

In this mating of rock and water, it was the water, softer and infinitely more pliable, who had her way, always shaping the rock to meet her own ends. Splashing down the granite walls, sometimes taking great leaps, then pausing to rest in the pools below, she sculpted and polished as she made her way down the watery path.

Jess led Susan to a spot Tim had described. They crossed the creek at a point marked by two boulders, each having the shape and features of a human face—if you used a little imagination. Between these two boulders a tributary creek ran into the one they had been following. This tributary creek was one of the crags' spillways. Tim had described this one as a "stairway to heaven," which offered increasingly spectacular vistas as you climbed upward.

Tim had also told them of a local legend, going back to the time of the earliest white settlements in the region. As the legend had it, the two boulders were the petrified remains of two brothers, members of a tribe of giants who'd lived thousands of years ago in the crags. These brothers had constantly quarreled and fought with each other. Their father had put up with this for as long as he could; finally, in a violent rage, he had thrown them bodily out of the house. They went tumbling down the spillway, their bodies torn to pieces as they bounced down the rocky pathway. Only their severed heads made it all the way down to the bottom of the spillway, and there they rest today.

Tim had added, "If you climb high enough, you'll see their ancient home."

So they climbed along the small creek, which grew steeper with each step. As they climbed, the flowing water was gradually transformed from a relatively placid mountain stream into something rougher, rawer, more elemental. The forest and the undergrowth receded, and the two climbers' line of sight extended all the way to the very tops of the crags. Here, there were few boulders or rocks of any sort lining the bottom of the watercourse—only the rushing, foaming water passing over smooth, polished rock.

They did pass one large black boulder standing by itself in the middle of the watercourse. A thin film of rushing water covered it, managing through a kind of liquid alchemy to transform the rock into a huge black gem, glistening in the sun.

In this barren, majestic landscape, all was rock and water, water and rock. It was the music of the eons, this sound of water rushing over rock.

As they climbed higher, they were rewarded with closeup views of the shimmering waterfalls. They appeared as silvery bands of sparkling water from afar, but up close one could see that they were a collection of cascading streamlets, and even these divided into thousands of shimmering droplets as one drew even closer—all of this somehow united in a beautiful cascading ballet of constant movement.

They were taking a rest while admiring a deep, dark-green pool at the bottom of one waterfall. Jess looked up and saw a massive, rectangular-shaped granite boulder perched on a ridge high above the waterfall. Its square corners had no counterpart in the roughly hewn crags above; it looked as if it had been dropped there from some other world. Or built by a race of giants . . .

As Jess and Susan hiked down from the crags that afternoon, they spoke little. Jess was awed by the experience; he could not even begin to put it into words. He had discovered a world that had remained essentially unchanged for millions of years. He had penetrated to the very center of things, had seen nature stripped down to the very core of its being.

It was as if he had entered a cathedral with a tourist's anticipation of stained glass windows and vaulted ceilings and polished wood and instead come face-to-face with God himself.

SNEAKING UP ON MOUNT SHASTA

Standing solitary and majestic in the Cascade Range, Mount Shasta at 14,162 feet dwarfs all the other mountains in its neighborhood. It is the defining landmark in my region, commanding the attention of travelers all the way from the Oregon border to the Sacramento Valley, 150 miles to the south. It is revered as a sacred mountain by Native Americans, Buddhists, New Agers and even a few Christian sects. And it poses a deceptively alluring challenge to all mountain climbers, experienced and novice alike.

From the staging area, at 6800 feet, the climb looks easy, perhaps a three- to four-hour effort. The slopes appear gentle and inviting. No ropes or other paraphernalia associated with technical climbing are required—just snow boots, crampons, an ice ax, and strong pairs of legs and lungs.

Before you head for its slopes, however, you should know that the mountain claims an average of one life per year and that there are countless other casualties due to falls and exposure to the elements. At the upper elevations, the mountain and the weather set parameters for the climb which are ever-changing and can lead to unpredictable difficulties. One summer a climber got himself stuck in a crevasse, not an unusual occurrence. Fortunately he got out uninjured, but his companion broke her back trying to dislodge him. A former student of mine tramped through forests for two days after

 heading down the wrong side of the mountain during a blinding snowstorm.

The great adventurer and naturalist John Muir was one of the first to try to lure all and sundry to the mountain's slopes. As you read his accounts describing his almost effortless conquest of Shasta, you have to keep in mind that this was a man whose idea of a good time was wallowing up to this armpits in snow and hopping over the yawning crevasses of Alaskan glaciers. Muir is probably the only snowbound climber on Mount Shasta ever to have expressed displeasure at being rescued.

In *Picturesque California*, published in 1888, he wrote, "During the bright days of midsummer the ascent of Shasta is only a long, safe saunter, without fright or nerve-strain, or even serious fatigue, to those in sound health."

If you want to see weary climbers smile, stand at Mount Shasta's staging area at the end of the day and ask those returning from the peak how their "saunter" went. Perhaps, with only slight exaggeration, the first few thousand feet of elevation gain could be described in that fashion, but very soon one finds that climbing on the mountain is like mounting the steps of a five-foot stepladder . . . over and over and over again. And after you've climbed those five steps you stop and gasp for breath.

I'm told that the last stretch of the climb on the main route isn't so bad, that the slope levels out somewhat and you've only got one potentially deadly crevasse to worry about.

Unfortunately, in several attempts, I've never gotten past the take-five-steps-and-gasp part. So this last summer I decided to try and outsmart the mountain. I was going to sneak up on it from the backside. There is a less frequently climbed side of the mountain that requires driving over 15 miles of winding dirt roads before you reach the jumping-off point. Last year a companion and I had scouted this route, and it certainly looked easy. Of course, so does the main route before you actually get on it, but this second route is generally considered the gentlest, easiest slope on the entire mountain by experienced guides. Horses have even been led up to the summit by this route.

So I started my climb on that side of the mountain in an optimistic mood. Setting out before dawn in the light of a full moon, I think I *was* almost sauntering. Sunrise found me taking communion from a deliciously cold, clear brooklet of water gushing from the mountain's interior.

Many hours later, above the snowline, I peered into a mist-blanketed fairyland. Tiny human figures draped themselves around the rocky spires of the summit. One of the little figures pranced around on a snowfield just below the summit. I was looking at the enchanted land one entered when the toil of climbing was over! But a glimpse of it was all I got. Soon after that the mists turned to clouds, reducing visibility to near-zero and threatening foul weather, and I was forced to descend.

Before I enjoyed that brief glimpse of a heavenly summit world, I had trudged for countless hours up the slope of the great mountain, in the slow drudgery of climbing, and the experience wasn't a whole lot different from that of the main route—i.e., climb and gasp, climb and gasp. Up and down the slopes on that day I could see other climbers who, like me, seemed to be spending as much time gazing wistfully upward as they did actually moving in that direction. You looked up and the summit seemed to be taunting you: "Here *I* am and *you're* still way down there."

To add to my difficulties, the rocky outcropping that I had been aiming toward all day and had assumed to be the summit, turned out to be several hundred feet below it, and was separated from the real one by a steep ice field. This unfortunate discovery, coupled with the above-mentioned change in the weather, convinced me that my climb was at an end.

So the mountain outsmarted me after all. But I'm not about to give up. That glimpse near the top only increased my desire to one day enter that enchanted summit world, one that seemed so far removed from the drudgery and fatigue of the world immediately below. If only I didn't have to climb a mountain to get there.

THE BIKE RIDE FROM HELL

*I*t all started out, as many ideas with disastrous consequences do, with a simple notion: Why don't the two of us, Pam and I, take a little three-day bike trip to the South Yuba River, near Nevada City, and camp out next to its cool green waters?

Fine. What's a little climb of 2000 feet or so? Both of us like exercise, and this was a chance to get some in while enjoying the pleasant scenery of the Sierra Nevada foothills. The route we would take was one I had bicycled many times: You start along the American River bike trail; pass through the towns of Loomis, Penryn, Newcastle, Auburn, and Nevada City; and end up on about 13 miles of hilly, winding backroads that lead you to your destination.

I will not bore the reader with sordid details here. Let's do a fast forward to mid-afternoon in Auburn, which finds Pam and me collapsed in a public park, the sounds of a baseball team in spring practice reaching our numbed senses. We had clearly overestimated our capacity for exercise, and had been forced to regroup for a lengthy snooze.

A good thing we did, too, because the day was still hot when we left Auburn around 4, plunging forward toward a roller-coaster succession of hills.

Without exaggeration, I think we each drank about two gallons

57

of water that day. Pausing at the top of a hill, we would gulp down the precious liquid, take a few deep breaths, and plunge bravely onward.

After a dozen or so hills, it became clear we would not make our planned campsite at the Yuba River. Nor would we make Nevada City. We rolled into Grass Valley about 7 p.m., had a sumptuous dinner at one of my favorite foothill restaurants, and camped out that night under the stars at the Nevada County fairgrounds. We both slept well.

That morning, leaving the fairgrounds, Pam's chain broke. We walked into town and discovered that Grass Valley's only bike shop had just gone out of business. However, as often happens in small towns, a good samaritan came to our rescue. Chris, an accountant whose wife runs a dress shop on Grass Valley's main street, offered to drive Pam and her bike to a bike shop in Nevada City. I followed behind on my bike.

At the bike shop, called Tour Of Nevada City, another very nice man fixed Pam's chain for free after displaying the incredibly stretched-out piece of equipment to admiring shop patrons. I used some of the shop tools to tighten my brakes, which had been giving me trouble. We also had to go back to a store down the road to buy a bolt to secure my bike rack, which had fallen off the day before.

So, in a state of blissful ignorance about the real mechanical condition of our bikes, especially mine, we spent a pleasant few hours in Nevada City, getting ready for the 13-mile trip to the Yuba River.

How could I have known, peacefully sipping coffee in a little Nevada City cafe, that I would soon be hurtling down the Yuba

River canyon, brakeless, desperately trying to use my tennis shoes as a form of emergency brake as I headed for oblivion? I stopped only because pressure from my outstretched left leg bent my saddlebag into the rear wheel's spokes. Amazingly, neither I nor the bike were permanently injured. Do I need to add that I walked the bike the rest of the way down to the river?

We spent the rest of the day rather pleasantly, I grateful to be alive, swimming in the river, reading, eating a leisurely dinner before snuggling into our sleeping bags on the sand.

Unfortunately, a renewed effort to tighten my brakes, which are old-fashioned ones using a Rube Goldberg-system of steel rods, turned out not to be successful, as I continued to hurtle down hills the next day, totally brakeless and out of control. I eventually got down the hill to Nevada City by literally dragging my feet alongside the bike and often walking down the really steep hills. We took a breather in Nevada City, and, proceeding cautiously, found a bike shop on the road to Grass Valley that was open on Sunday.

There, at Samurai Bikes (an ominous name), was a lone employee, a combination salesman/repairman who appeared to be all of 14 years old and who identified himself as "Samurai Bob." He turned out to be a very competent young mechanic. After attempting an ingenious brake repair method that involved twisting a spoke around, under and through my convoluted brake system, Samurai Bob settled for simply tightening the existing system with all his might.

Although this did not result in a total restoration of my brakes, it was enough to slow me down considerably on the steep hills for the rest of the trip. Pam, who had been having trouble braking also, replaced her rear brake shoes.

Still proceeding with caution, we made it to Auburn by 6, and by 9 p.m. the sign in front of the Orangevale Assembly of God church was welcoming us, although we decided not to stop.

We continued pleasantly enough by moonlight—oh, except for the two flat tires I got on Hazel Avenue just before heading back on the American River bike trail. On the trail we were stopped and questioned by a park ranger, who wanted to know why we were on the bike trail at that hour. ("It's a long story, officer . . .")

Well, we made it back in one piece, more or less. Pam is hoping that the poison oak rash that has crept over her arms and legs won't last too long, and me, I just look at those long stretches of flat road around Sacramento with a new sense of appreciation.

MIND-JOGGING AT OCEAN BEACH

*I*t's a good day to go mind-jogging at Ocean Beach, on the sandy western shore of San Francisco. It's one of those clear, crisp winter days when everything is painted in broad swaths of colors: gray sand, green water, pale-blue sky. Way out at sea a Navy aircraft carrier drifts westward. The ship looks fragile, unreal.

I like to run where the sand is moist and springy, so I skirt along the surf's edge, playing tag with the waves that come rolling up the shore. As I run alongside the surf, I can feel the rhythm of the sea. Instinctively, I absorb its tempo; I dart in and out among the waves without even thinking about it.

The usual crowd is scattered about the beach. Old men, youthful drifters, a few couples. I notice when I glance toward the sea wall that old George is working his diggings again. George hunts for buried treasure at Ocean Beach. The way George tells it, there's a virtual fortune in jewelry and coins buried in the sand, waiting for anyone who has the time and patience to claim it. Every lost ring and every piece of change that slips out of someone's pocket remains there on the beach. Each year, as the sand is washed back and forth by the tide, the tiny metal objects sink deeper and deeper, eventually clustering around buried rocks and wooden pilings.

George does his treasure hunting with a garden spade. It takes patience, something which George seems to have plenty of. He claims to have unearthed a diamond ring once. Gold pieces, too. He fishes into his pocket and shows me the day's booty: 52 cents in change and a gold ring. Not bad, considering the change included an 1891 Liberty Head nickel—lost, perhaps, by some unfortunate picnicker 80 years ago.

We are an odd assortment, we beach habitues. The beach seems to attract the very old and the very young. People, judging from the looks of them, whose chief asset is leisure time. Even though we are all beach dwellers on a purely temporary basis, there's a sense of community here. We are all drawn by the special lure of the ocean. Some want to touch it, to feel its chilly waters creep up around their bodies as they wade out from shore. Most are content to sit quietly on the beach and ponder it at a respectful distance.

I try to be a good neighbor to my fellow beach habitues. I am careful to avoid trodding on the occasional jellyfish that gets stranded on the beach. I give the flocks of seabirds a wide berth, to avoid frightening them. I am on nodding terms with the young seal who goes fishing in the kelp beds when the tide is low. I am friendly, too, with the old fisherman who works the other side of the shoreline at low tide.

These two, the seal and the fisherman, are an odd pair. Neither is really much interested in fish. The seal is young and frisky and makes a great show of diving in and out among the waves, supposedly searching for something to fill his stomach. But he doesn't fool me. All that splashing about is simply his way of taking a little holiday from nearby Seal Rock. It can't be easy living on a tiny island with all your relatives and former lovers.

The fisherman is old and goes about his business in a more relaxed way than the seal. He plants a sturdy stake in the sand, straps his pole to it, and squats down to wait. He sits there for hours, hugging his knees and gazing seaward. Philoso-fishing, you could call it. I think he is better at philosophizing than fishing. At least I have never seen him pull anything out of the water other than what he put there in the first place.

Still, the fishline may serve as a trail for his mind to follow, a pathway down to the waters below where his thoughts can rest, undisturbed, just like the bait at the end of his hook. And the line and hook may serve as a mental anchor, to keep his thoughts from drifting too far out to sea.

"Any luck yet?" I always ask when I see him.

"Not yet," he replies. "The water's too high," he says one day. "The wind's too strong," he says the next, or, "it's too cold." During all the time I've been jogging, the weather's never been quite right. You have to be patient to fish at Ocean Beach.

The seagulls and the pigeons, roughly speaking, form the right and left-wing factions of the bird population. The seagulls don't especially like other birds sharing their feeding grounds, especially low-class, low-rent, inner-city pigeons. The seagulls seem to feel they own the entire beach. The pigeons, naturally, figure they've got as much right to be on the beach as anyone else.

So the two of them are constantly at odds. I have seen seagull neighborhoods transformed into all-pigeon neighborhoods in a matter of minutes. One or two scruffy-looking pigeons appear on the scene and a whole flock of seagulls stalks off in a huff.

The sandpipers have stayed aloof from the controversy thus far. They seem content to share the beach with both seagulls and pigeons alike. They are the liberal-minded members of the bird population.

One afternoon my mind was jogged in a pleasant direction by the sight of a lovely young woman doing a spontaneous dance among the waves near the shore. A sizeable crowd had gathered on the beach, and in front of this spontaneous audience she danced, fully clothed, among the waves—her long flowing hair, indeed her whole body, swaying to the rhythm of the ocean.

THE TIM HOLT DAM

*T*his is the story of how a dam came to be built. This dam will not rank as one of the great feats of human engineering, along the lines of a Grand Coulee or a Bonneville. No, the Tim Holt Dam is a modest little dam. It is a joint project of the city of Dunsmuir and yours truly and consists of three sturdy sandbags supplied by the city and dirt and rocks supplied by myself. It is three feet wide and about a foot high.

The Tim Holt Dam, unlike its better-known counterparts here in the Northwest, does not generate electricity, nor do tourists come to gawk at it. But it does serve a purpose that neither the Bonneville nor the Grand Coulee can boast of: When its modest reservoir is dry, the neighborhood kids can use the Tim Holt Dam as a launch ramp for their bicycles.

How did this dam come to be built? Well, I have a neighbor who about a year ago began building his own home just up the street from me. The home site is carved at the base of a bare cliff with little vegetation. He started building his home this past winter, and the heavy rains washed a good deal of the bare site down the gutter and into the nearby Sacramento River. As the work progressed, diluted cement and paint were also washed down.

I spoke with him about using erosion control measures, such as straw bales, but no such steps were taken. Finally, on a day when he was hosing down the front of the property, and sending more sediment down the street, I took action. The first version of the Tim Holt Dam took about 20 minutes to build, but it worked, effectively halting the flow of mud. The next day, after a car or truck had run over it, it had to be rebuilt. Then the city stepped into the picture. A Public Works employee assigned to trim shrubbery along a public walkway near our home and generally clean up the neighborhood also shoveled most of the Tim Holt Dam into the back of his pickup before I could get down to the street to stop him. When I did get down and explained the dam's purpose, he proposed the use of some of the city's sandbags: neater and more official-looking.

I have had to rebuild the dam a number of times since then, mostly due to its use as a bicycle launch ramp. Folks walking or driving by when I'm out working on my dam may wonder why I'm engaged in such an activity, and, yes, I do feel a little silly at such times, for the connection between my little dam and the health of the river's fish isn't obvious. But it is satisfying, when the water behind the dam subsides, to scoop the dirt up that has accumulated behind the dam and haul it up to my compost pile, for I know this is dirt that will not end up clogging the riverbed and the spawning sites of our local trout.

When I first started building my dam, the homebuilder's wife, watching me from a distance as I shoveled dirt, called out an apology for the "mess" their home construction was causing and promised it would soon be at an end.

She, of course, was concerned about the appearance of the immediate neighborhood. As I get older, I'm finding that my own concept of neighborhood keeps expanding.

WOLVES AT THE DOOR

I'm looking forward to the return of the wolves to their historic range in the West. For that matter, they're welcome right in my backyard; they might keep those pesky deer from chomping on my swiss chard.

An estimated 20 wolves have swum across the Snake River from Idaho—where record numbers of federally protected wolf pups were born this past denning season—to check out hunting prospects in Oregon. Since wolves can travel as much as 500 miles on their scouting trips, it's virtually inevitable that the first gray wolf will soon return to its ancestors' old stomping grounds in the upper reaches of California's mountain ranges. (The last one to inhabit California was killed in a remote part of Lassen County in 1924.)

The prospect of the wolves' return has caused an uproar among livestock owners and their political representatives in my home territory. The Siskiyou County Board of Supervisors, whose rural domain will likely be one of the gateways for the wolves, has passed a resolution opposing the return of the wolf, and, in particular, any effort to "introduce or reintroduce" the wolf to the

This article first appeared in the San Francisco Chronicle *on September 15, 2002.*

county. The supervisors were reacting to a petition by Defenders of Wildlife asking the federal government to study southern Oregon and Northern California as prime locations for restored wolf populations.

The wolves, of course, could care less about any resolutions or petitions; they'll come in their own good time to look around and, if the hunting's good, attempt to settle here. When they do, they will no doubt encounter the "shoot, shovel and shut up" creed of rural resistors to the Endangered Species Act.

After all, there's an historic tradition to maintain: The bighorn sheep, the wolverine, and the wolf have all been killed off or driven from the region. With the construction of Shasta and other dams the wild salmon has been all but eliminated, too. A few remnants of the once-thriving herds of antelope still survive on the north slopes of Mount Shasta. Of the larger game animals, only the elk and the deer remain in anything like significant numbers.

For the past 150 years in these regions and throughout the West we have taken it for granted that the entry of our own species into a region takes precedence over all other living things. The re-entry of the wolf will test whether we have evolved beyond this narrow-minded attitude.

Hopefully we've begun to realize that our dominance over the rest of the living world has been a sterile victory. Joaquin Miller's mid-19th century descriptions of the Mount Shasta region portray a land teeming with wildlife, of streams "so filled with salmon that it was impossible to force a horse across the current" and long lines of deer and other game animals threading their way along mountain passages. Now, when I hike these same mountains, I'm lucky if I see an occasional bird or squirrel.

The re-entry of the wolf provides a pure litmus test of our commitment to restoring our lost wilderness for its own sake. When we restore salmon habitat, there are obvious and direct benefits to humans, but the benefits to be derived from the wolf can only be measured in the wilds.

And they are considerable. Wolf re-entry to the wilderness is good news for all wild species, with the possible exception of its main competitor, the coyote. Wolves strengthen the stock of other animal populations, like deer and elk, by feeding on the weak and old. By doing so, they also help prevent the depletion of natural vegetation. And their kills provide leftover meals for foxes, bears and raptors, among others.

It's true that livestock owners would suffer the most from wolf re-introduction. To ease their burden, Defenders of Wildlife is funding cooperative programs with ranchers in the Rocky Mountain states and the Southwest. In those states Defenders has contributed funds to help ranchers purchase electric fencing, guard dogs, and even cowboy security guards to protect cattle herds and sheep from wolves. In Arizona livestock owners who have cooperated with wolf re-entry programs—for example, by carefully guarding or fencing their cattle or sheep when wolf dens are nearby—can put "predator-friendly" labels on their products to enhance consumer appeal, an approach that could certainly reap benefits for meat producers in California.

Defenders has also set up a trust fund to pay livestock owners for killings by wolves, and it has offered to extend this program to California.

The entry of wolves into the western states (Canadian wolves have already made their way into Washington) is occurring against a shifting and ominous political backdrop. Currently the federal government is backing off from wolf protection, a policy that is leaving some western states, particularly Oregon, in the lurch.

Under considerable pressure from livestock interests, the U.S. Fish And Wildlife Service wants to take the wolf off the Endangered Species list in California, Nevada, Washington and Oregon. The feds argue that they have done their part on behalf of the beleaguered animal by establishing viable wolf populations in the Rocky Mountain states, and that it is now up to the rest of the western states to decide what they're going to do with any of the four-legged immigrants that may cross their borders.

That argument has some merit, but the federal government's timing is at best irresponsible and at worst malevolent, given that Oregon has barely begun the process of coming up with a wolf management plan and California hasn't even started. In the meantime, the feds' action can only give comfort to the "shoot, shovel and shutup" crowd.

And let's not kid ourselves about our own state government taking any leadership role here. Its efforts on behalf of the wild salmon have been tepid at best, as proposals for effective watershed restoration have been repeatedly watered down by opposition from the timber industry. Can anyone imagine our pay-to-play governor, Gray Davis, sticking his neck out for a bunch of four-legged carnivores who don't carry checkbooks?

California's wild salmon have some hope for recovery only because of the efforts of thousands of volunteers working through watershed restoration groups throughout Northern California (including some of the same Siskiyou County ranchers who are currently howling for the wolves' return). Support for the wolf must also come from the grassroots, hopefully with cooperation from livestock owners via the incentives mentioned above.

Nowadays we give a lot of lip service to the need to preserve and protect the wilds. The return of the wolves will test whether we really mean it.

BEYOND THE BUBBLE

This is another excerpt from my novel On Higher Ground. *The year is 2047. William and Cheryl Shawntree have left the climate-controlling dome of Sacramento, where, due to global warming and rampant pollution, all air coming into the dome has to be purified and cooled. They have moved to the more pristine environs of Mount Shasta, where they can still live under open skies and breathe clean, unfiltered air. Five years after their move, as he bustles about their farm doing daily chores, William is musing about the changes in his and Cheryl's lives since they left Sacramento.*

*T*he Bubble People, that's how William thought of the people they had left behind in Sacramento. It was, to be sure, a smug, self-congratulatory term, and a little hypocritical, since he and Cheryl had spent seven years inside that bubble. But somehow they had found the will and the energy to pull up stakes, to leave the bubble and start a life up here. At first they had felt exhilarated, and at the same time frighteningly naked and vulnerable, to look up and see the stars at night and the sun and the blue sky and the clouds during the day.

Yes, they were pioneers in a way, but not because they bathed in iron tubs or scrubbed their clothes on washboards. No, their life for the most part was just as comfortable as it had been in the city.

They were pioneers, in their city friends' eyes, because they had ventured into the threatening Unknown, into the world beyond the dome.

In their own eyes, they were pioneers because they were attempting to wrest a living from the land and from the sweat of their brows.

The Shawntrees had moved onto a former ranch, a 50-acre spread framed by the two imposing giants of the landscape—Mount Eddy to the west and Mount Shasta on the east. It was one big meadow when they moved there, with a small forest of trees in the northwest corner. It and the neighboring spreads had been used early in the last century as the setting for Western movies, starring a long-forgotten cowboy actor named Tom Mix, and when you looked out from the house across the fields, with those imposing mountains in the background, you could see why Hollywood had favored this mountain valley, known locally as the Strawberry Valley. The soft, inviting beauty of Nature, as well as her threatening, intimidating side, were combined in one magnificent vista. When the sky was laced with lightning during one of the frequent winter thunderstorms, and the trees undulated, one after another, marking the passage of the wind through the forest, and the grasses bowed down in waves before the force of that same wind, why, then you felt that Nature herself had taken over the direction and staging of her own spectacular drama.

It was, in all respects, as different a world as you could imagine from that in Sacramento.

When they had first moved to the ranch, William and Cheryl had no idea how to go about making a living. Somewhere in the

back of their minds was the slowly germinating idea that they could make some sort of living from the land, but at first they, like other emigres before them, tried to replicate the jobs they'd had in the city. For Cheryl, that meant taking temporary office jobs that usually involved glorified secretarial work, and not always glorified at that. Government jobs were hard to come by, unless you wanted to commute long distances, so William got a part-time job teaching English at the local community college.

They had managed to keep a small garden plot in the city and had continued the practice up here, albeit in a space much larger than the city plot. The first year they had simply grown a small amount of green and yellow and orange stuff in the summer, but by the following year they had built a greenhouse and were trucking produce down to the farmers' markets in Dunsmuir and Mt. Shasta.

They had been able to scrape together the mortgage payments in their first year, but with their gradual plunge into full-time farming the payments soon got whittled down to the bare minimum.

And then the phone calls from the bank's loan officer, Tom Griffiths, started coming, every month or so. The difficulty lay in finding a good cash crop, one that would provide reliable and abundant harvests year after year and fetch premium prices at the farmers' markets and in direct sales to restaurants and other produce buyers throughout the region and down in the valley.

But as they struggled with the business side of farming, they were already reaping benefits from this new life that were not reflected in their bank balance. Slowly in the fresh mountain air and under vibrant blue skies they began to re-invent themselves and their lives. In the city, work had been something they did so that they could afford to do other, more enjoyable things, or so they could buy the things they thought they needed. Up here, as they gradually spent more and more of their time in the fields, work became not a means to an end but an end in itself. Work in the soil, the hoeing and the turning over of the earth, the sowing of seeds and the planting of seedlings, and then the reward of the harvest—all of this was recreation in the usual sense of the word, as their tanned and trimmer bodies attested, but it was re-*creation* as well, a central part of the ongoing evolution of their lives. And as the work in the fields became an end in itself, something to be enjoyed and savored, the Shawntrees found that they were willing to shed things from their past life that no longer seemed important. Their combined income, what they were able to scrape together after the bank received its minimum tithe, was no more than one-fifth what it had been in the city, but they saw their reduced circumstances as a fair price to pay for the joy of living in this beautiful area and the chance to do work that actually enriched their lives.

A FREEWAY COMES TO LIFE

In this excerpt from On Higher Ground, *Jess Renfree, a refugee from the Sacramento dome, takes his first trip on the old Interstate 5 freeway near Mount Shasta. By the year 2047, skyrocketing oil prices have ushered in a new era of transportation, vastly more diverse and colorful than that of the present age.*

*B*orrowing a bicycle from the Shawntrees, Jess set out early one morning toward the little town of Dunsmuir, about ten miles to the south. He pedaled to the old interstate freeway that connected the town of Mt. Shasta with Dunsmuir. He headed up an onramp and was suddenly confronted with a varied and confusing array of travelers, each of them seeming to have his or her own unique mode of transportation. Some walked, some skated, some rode skateboards, and some, like Jess, bicycled. There were quite a few travelers on horseback and even some horse-drawn wagons. These, and an occasional slow-moving auto or truck or bus, occupied the center lanes, while the human-powered transportation moved along in the outer lanes. The hikers tended to stay on the very outer edges of the old freeway, to avoid the faster-moving traffic.

Jess soon found himself weaving in and out among the skaters and slower bicyclists. It was rather like being in the middle of a traveling street fair from the Middle Ages. All around there was the sound of chattering voices, clattering hooves, the occasional cry of an infant. Most of the horse-drawn wagons pulled some kind of merchandise. Often it was yellow or green or red produce of some sort, but Jess also saw what appeared to be handmade wooden toys in the bed of one wagon, and piles of thickly woven throw rugs in another. Another wagon was filled with round metal containers—probably milk, Jess thought—and another with bales of hay.

Some of the bicyclists even carried goods behind them in small trailers. Jess saw one bearded, middle-aged fellow with a heavy load of books, and a young woman with a colorful assortment of kites.

Jess realized after awhile that there was a crazy, patchwork pattern to the traffic on this highway. Those using human-powered, wheeled transportation—skaters, skate-boarders, and bicyclists—tended to follow one another in narrow, winding rivulets, and these individual rivulets wound around and sometimes through one another, frequently adjusting their course to avoid stray pedestrians. The overall effect was like that produced by a kaleidoscope, with swirling, ever-changing patterns of motion and color.

Many of the bicyclists had attached long, colorful streamers of ribbons to the rear of their bikes and trailers. Bright, multi-colored jerseys were popular attire, and both men and women favored form-fitting leggings, or leotards in colors ranging from black to the brightest yellows and reds.

Perhaps because of the small number of motor-driven vehicles, few of the cyclists wore helmets. In their place, all kinds of headgear were in evidence: sunbonnets, beanies with propellers, berets and the more prosaic baseball or fishing caps. One fellow wearing a top hat and vintage 19th century garb, which included a long-tailed coat, sailed by on a big-wheeled bicycle. From his lofty perch he acknowledged greetings from the crowd below with a dignified nod of the head.

Only the center lane, with its heavier, lumbering vehicles, each traveling a straight trajectory, suggested the freeway of a bygone era. The rest of the thoroughfare, with its swirling and interweaving streams of traffic, bore more resemblance to the nearby river that meandered down the canyon it had carved through the mountains, the canyon the freeway builders had followed, and the railway-builders before them. The freeway, it seemed, was returning to its roots.

THE WORLD
OF PRINT

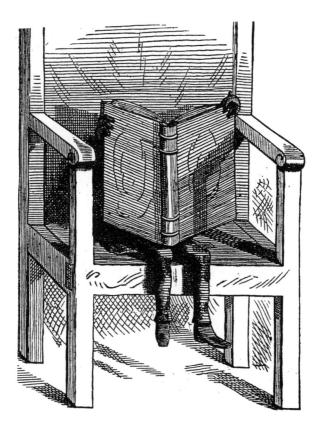

CONFESSIONS OF A PRINT ADDICT

*A*s I write this, I am sitting at our kitchen table surrounded by piles of books, notes for articles, and other print ephemera. To my left is a tottering pile of partially read magazines and newspapers. I am constantly telling myself that I will whittle it down inch by inch. This is not impossible, for I can pretty well sail through the ad-choked *New York Times Magazine* and, in *The New Yorker*, plow through the cartoons and perhaps one or two worthwhile articles. But then I hit *The New York Review Of Books*, thick and dense with ideas, and in the time it takes me to wade through it the pile begins to grow again.

The fact is I like being surrounded by print, by this silent babble of voices, any one of which, whenever I choose, can be called upon to enlighten and entertain me.

I am in fact a hopeless print addict, with no intention of ever trying to rid myself of the habit.

It all started innocently enough. I remember hurrying home from school, over forty years ago, to read those great yarns of childhood, *Treasure Island* and *Twenty Thousand Leagues Under The Sea.* I do not remember many of the books I checked out from the local library, but I do remember their bindings, those standard library covers in soft creamy pastel colors, the colors of candy kisses and salt water taffy.

By the early '60s I was beginning to move beyond the soft literary confections of childhood. One summer in my early teens I luxuriated in the warm, languid and (as I recall) mildly erotic prose of James Michener's *Hawaii.* And during another languorous summer I was able to follow with a political neophyte's avid interest the intrigues of Allen Drury's *Advise And Consent.*

So at an early age I embraced reading as one of life's great pleasures, always available, always at my beck and call, undemanding, seductive, and thoroughly addictive.

In those early years, during Sacramento's hot suburban summers, I spent carefree hours not only reading but also swimming and golfing and playing tennis. But as often happens in life, something came along to shake me out of this complacent and pleasant existence. I discovered girls. The resulting explorations into the mysteries of the opposite sex, coupled with the increasing demands of school, seemed to leave little time for pleasure reading.

Despite the strains of this unsettled period, I look back on that time—the high school years and early years of college—with a kind of wistful regret. For this was the one and only time in my life that I was following a sensible trajectory that would have likely led toward marriage, children and a respectable job.

I don't know whether it was serendipity or fate, but it *is* certain that my life took a permanent detour from its relatively safe and predictable path the day I picked up, from a revolving rack at the supermarket, a paperback edition of Carlos Baker's biography of Ernest Hemingway.

I was then at a crossroads. I was in my early twenties with no clear idea of what sort of career I wanted to pursue. This book, with its lurid red cover and seductive contents, seemed to say: Why not be a writer, pursue adventure all over the world, write bestselling novels, and sip aperitifs in dark cafes with others of the bohemian *demi-monde*? For an impressionable young man highly susceptible to the allure of the print world, it was altogether the worst book I could possibly have read.

In the ensuing years, try as I might to follow in his footsteps, my life was but a pale shadow of the Great Writer's. I attended my first and only bullfight in Mexico City, a disgusting spectacle that left me rooting for the bull. For several months I sat myself down at my desk every morning, like my role model, and wrote short stories, but they were raw and unpublishable, and I never submitted them anywhere.

I finally did cross paths with Mr. Hemingway and some of his literary pals, at least in spirit. It was in Paris during the summer of 1973, while the U.S. was in the throes of the Watergate crisis. I stayed for a few days in a book-lined apartment above Paris's famed Shakespeare and Company bookstore. Out my window Notre Dame loomed over the rooftops of Paris. An autographed photo of James Joyce greeted me as I mounted the stairs to the living quarters. (The bookstore's founder, Sylvia Beach, had launched Joyce's career by publishing *Ulysses*.) Among the store's first customers had been Ernest Hemingway, F. Scott Fitzgerald, Thornton Wilder, and Gertrude Stein.

By the time I came upon it, the store, the only English-language bookshop in Paris, had been taken over by a kindhearted and eccentric older man who, if he took a liking to you, would invite you to stay upstairs in exchange for doing odd jobs around the store. So I communed with the spirits of some of the great writers of the 20th century while repairing shelves by day and gazing out my window at night at Victor Hugo's grand cathedral. The fact that there were bedbugs in the sheets was a small price to pay for the other, more exalted company I kept at Shakespeare and Company.

My month-long sojourn in France was followed by a short and uncertain and unprofitable period as a freelance journalist in the San Francisco Bay Area, followed by a long and unprofitable period publishing a cash-starved weekly newspaper back in Sacramento. (See "My Life As A Publisher," page 99.) My path, to say the least, had by then diverged widely from that of my role model's. I was too busy selling ads, delivering papers and interviewing city officials to do much fishing for marlin in the Gulf Stream or hunting for lions in Africa. I was lucky, after the paper folded, just to hold onto my house.

Did this cure me? Not at all. In my adult life, I had evolved from a passive to an active print addict, a disseminator as well as a user of the stuff, and I was not about to be stopped by the collapse of my newspaper after a run of 19 years. In fact, if anything I plunged even deeper into the abyss.

As the newspaper was going under, I set out to publish a book on Sacramento's history, typesetting it on an old linotype machine and printing it, sheet by sheet, on a handfed letterpress. (See next chapter.) I had a lot of time on my hands in those days; the task involved, I once calculated, feeding more than 30,000 sheets of paper into the press to print just 200 copies of the book. I went home each night with ink-stained hands, the ink, I am sure, finding its way inexorably into my blood.

I have since published four more books, including this one, all using updated computer technology. Now, in my role as small-time book publisher, I haunt bookstores to see how my books are displayed, and I sell them through readings and book-signings and other shameless promotional efforts, whenever and however I can.

Like most long-time addicts, I can always find excuses and rationalizations for my behavior. As a publisher of books, I prefer to think of myself not as an addict-pusher, but in the more refined role of *purveyor*—the print version of a wine merchant, who provides a product that can either be enjoyed in moderation or consumed to the point of stupification and ruin, all depending on the user. Or so I tell myself.

Would I recommend a life devoted to the printed word, to devouring it, printing it, publishing it, and living off the meager proceeds it typically provides? Would I recommend to young people that they shut themselves off from sunny, sociable paths and pursue the life of the writer and bookworm? Of course not. Would I choose any other life? Certainly not.

HOT TYPE

*I*n this secular age, I am committing the closest thing possible to sacrilege. I am using, even reveling in, a discarded technology. When I set out to publish my first book, I turned my back on the all-seeing, all-knowing beneficence of the computer, and opted instead for the messy but exacting art of letterpress printing.

Each page I print is hand fed to the waiting jaws of a 70-year-old press. The press run is counted, not in brightly lit digital numbers, but on raised metal letters that advance with the rhythm of the press. Each night I come home with hands so deeply stained with ink that nothing will get them clean. But unlike Lady McBeth, I am proud to display them as a badge of my hands-on dedication to this craft.

With modern, computer-driven publishing, you are dealing with the two dimensions of the computer screen. In letterpress printing the third dimension is there with a vengeance. Just one of my chapters, preserved on about 100 small bars of lead, weighs 25 pounds. The entire book, all 130 pages worth, weighs over 500 pounds.

It is a weighty tome indeed, a fact made all too clear one day when two shelves of type, containing three chapters, fell crashing to the floor. Since each line of type reads backwards, putting it all

Linotype machine. © 1978 Allan Jones Studios, Sacramento.

back together was like doing a crossword puzzle in Arabic. But for someone who's always been fascinated by the printed word, there's a deep satisfaction in being able to actually hold the type in my hand and to place each line in a printer's form, ready to be inked and pressed to the paper.

The book, by the way, is a history of my hometown, Sacramento, California, written by a Mr. Lloyd Bruno, an emigré from Colorado who taught English and journalism at the local community college.

Working in spurts, usually about one day a week, it took me two years to typeset the book. This was done on a huge, 3000-pound mechanical monster called a linotype. Developed in the late 19th century and used by most newspapers until the middle of the 20th century, it is an ingenious but mechanically temperamental device; its frequent breakdowns resulted in union rules in some shops that required one mechanic on duty for every four linotypes in operation.

It is awe-inspiring to watch this behemoth select, cast, and redistribute type. Letter molds squeezed together to form each line of the book's text are waltzed through a series of delicate operations. After hot lead has been pressed into the molds to form the raised letters necessary for printing, each letter mold must be returned to its proper storage slot. To accomplish this, a huge arm descends from the upper reaches of the machine. It plucks up the line of molds and redistributes each one down its particular storage chute to rest with molds of the same letter.

One hardly expects a machine of this size, with its huge moving parts, to do such precise work. It is a little like watching an elephant dance a credible version of "The Nutcracker."

As one might expect from an aging machine with several hundred moving parts and a very precise mission to fulfill, things do go wrong. During my first few months of typesetting, I spent many an hour crawling around the machine's base searching for letter molds it had inexplicably spit out. In what must have been an expression of contempt for my ineptitude, one day the linotype shot a jet of hot lead at me, hitting the back of my right hand. (The scar from that accident, like my ink-stained hands, I would proudly show off for months to come.)

As this is being written, I am involved in the lengthy task of feeding each page of the book into the press by hand. All in all, that's over 30,000 hand feeds. And each freshly inked sheet must be scrutinized for defects—inadvertent fingerprints and spots caused by dust or lint are the most common glitches—and then stacked carefully, with a clean sheet in between each inked one, in a cardboard box.

Why am I using this time-consuming method of printing when the book could be produced in much less time using modern printing techniques? Well, part of the reason is precisely that the old way *is* time-consuming. In this hurried age, I am luxuriating in time, substituting my time and labor for the operations of a computer and an offset press. And so I have the satisfaction of knowing that each page of the book is all the more my work: the result of my labor, my attention to details, my decisions about ink levels, roller pressure, press speed and dozens of other variables. My reward is a pride of craftsmanship known to anyone who makes their own clothes, their own pottery, their own furniture.

In an era when we humans are apparently being voice-mailed, computerized, and automated out of the labor force, making something by hand is a quiet act of rebellion.

BOOK PEDALING

I am that humble toiler in the literary world, the self-published author. The connotation of "self-published" is, of course, "couldn't find a real publisher." But let's not forget that Whitman couldn't find a real publisher for *Leaves Of Grass,* nor could Joyce for *Ulysses.* Pioneering works that are not readily marketable—or written under the watchful eye of repressive regimes—must often find channels outside the mainstream, whether xeroxed, passed from hand to hand, or self-published.

Now, I like to think that my work is daringly original and not without literary merit, but I don't claim to be the next Whitman or Joyce just by virtue of being self-published. The fact is, I *like* being self-published for its own sake. I like having the final say over the contents and the covers of my books. As a small-time entrepreneur, I like dealing directly with small owner-operated bookstores. And, although they haven't been clamoring for my books lately, I take especial delight in thumbing my nose at Barnes and Noble and Borders and Amazon.com—those impersonal behemoths of the book world.

As a self-publisher I revel in the little victories. I am competing, after all, with the thousands of new books that come out each year, most of them from publishers with substantially more resources than mine. Getting my books into the hands of a paying bookstore customer often requires persistence and patience. Case in point: The manager of a bookstore in Oakland reads a sample copy of my novel, *On Higher Ground*, doesn't like the characters, rejects it. Two years later a new manager takes over. I drop off the book when I'm in town. She misplaces it. I send her another one. Perhaps partly out of guilt she agrees to display it prominently in the store. It sells in two weeks.

For me, no cross-country book tours, no luxury hotel suites. I pedal down from the Mount Shasta region on my bicycle every six months or so to promote my books in Sacramento and the Bay Area and some of the small towns of the foothills. In San Francisco and the East Bay, I cycle from bookstore to bookstore, with an occasional author talk thrown in along the way. I stay in a friend's cramped basement apartment in the Sunset District—the home of a fellow print addict, where stacks of newspapers and magazines compete with the furniture for precious space. I provision myself from the local natural foods store and nearby Chinese groceries.

Since one of my major themes is simple living, this seems an appropriate way to go about promoting and distributing my books. And since I am not distributing books by the hundreds or thousands, the bicycle mode works just fine. I am the literary equivalent of one of those pushcart vendors of an earlier era who pedaled his wares door to door. The books ride behind me in a pair of baskets, each lined with faded blue tarpaulin to keep them clean and dry. For the long haul down from Mount Shasta, I hook on my bike trailer with sleeping bag and tent and cooking gear.

Not the way Calvin Trillin or Garry Wills does it, I'm sure. But I dwell in a very different world from theirs. In the Bay Area I operate in the deep shadows cast by the likes of Caroline Kennedy and Jimmy Carter. I don't know what it's like for other authors, but for me the Bay Area can be a kind of black hole: Phone calls go unreturned; books disappear from the shelves or are somehow lost in shipment, and then, like wayward asteroids, magically reappear again.

While the major authors make their appearances at places like A Clean Well-Lighted Place and Cody's, I must seek my audiences at libraries, community colleges, and the like.

But these more intimate settings can have their own special charms. I think back to an appearance a few years ago, a luncheon talk at the Berkeley City Commons Club in an elegant old Julia Morgan Building near the university. The room where I spoke, on one of the upper floors of the building, was more parlor than lecture hall, a perfect Edith Wharton setting: Gleaming silverware, white tablecloths, book-lined walls, a fireplace behind the lectern. It was an elderly audience, for the most part—retired professors, retired executives, one retired Army colonel. They looked up from their plates of salmon with keen, alert faces. After I had given my talk there were the politely worded but pointed questions—challenging, among other things, the philosophy of simple living and Henry Thoreau's lifestyle—all manner of thoughtful questions delivered with the characteristic graciousness of their generation.

In one of the loneliest of professions, this is the supreme reward. In those few moments of spirited give-and-take the intangible relationship between writer and audience crystallized into something almost tangible. In those few moments, in those gilded surroundings, I felt as if I'd arrived at the center of the impulse for writing and, yes, for self-publishing.

MY LIFE AS A PUBLISHER

I came home to Sacramento in 1974. Downtown Sacramento at that time was a small town within the city that came to life for about half an hour each weekday, when thousands of state government employees sought their midday meal. Once the sun set each day, barely a soul stirred on the city's streets. With the exception of a few bars and one espresso coffee house, nothing was open anyway. Folks sequestered themselves in the evenings in suburban enclaves spread out for miles to the south, north and east of town.

Such a vacuum presents opportunities. There were dilapidated buildings in that vacuum, and that meant low rents. Low rents attracted a wide range of folks, many of us young, at loose ends and ready to do some experimenting with our lives. Some were artists. Others, like myself, had no creative pretensions but were at that young and dangerous stage when we had nothing to lose—no mortgaged homes, no dependent family, no career.

There is a Teutonic strain in Sacramento's psyche, one that emphasizes playing strictly by the rules, resists change and is focused on the tangible and concrete as opposed to the spiritual and creative side of human existence. This Teutonic strain was evident when a few brave restaurateurs tried to bring a little European flavor to the state's capital by placing tables out on sidewalks in the

This article was first published in 1994.

mid-1970s. There was an outcry from City Hall about the impediments this would create for pedestrians. Never mind that in Paris, where they actually *do* have pedestrians in significant numbers, you don't see people stumbling over sidewalk furniture.

The challenge to this straightlaced mindset would come, in the 1970s, from a downtown community inhabited not only by artists and writers but also by alternative-style entrepreneurs who set up crafts stores, restaurants, coffee houses and art galleries. They were joined by more solid, mainstream types, mostly state workers, who aimed for an elegant House Beautiful existence in rehabbed downtown Victorians. These Old City Association pioneers soon discovered they could only realize their dream by battling City Hall—at first, over restrictive city building codes that made no allowances for the quirks of older homes, and later over broader quality-of-life issues such as traffic congestion.

I jumped into this scene as an ex-busboy just fired from an Old Sacramento restaurant for punching the head waiter. I had $6000 in the bank and no entanglements, personal or professional. What the hell, why not follow up on a friend's suggestion to start a newspaper in Sacramento? All you had to do was walk into Giovanni's coffeehouse (later renamed Weatherstone), Julianna's Kitchen or Mickey Abbey's stained glass studio or stroll by the half-acre of community gardens at 15th and Q streets to feel that something new was happening here.

So I signed a month-to-month rental agreement on a second floor "office" (formerly a one-bedroom apartment) at 18th and L streets. After painting over the previous tenants' crayon drawings and figuring out how to operate the Murphy bed, I had a very inexpensive office and living space. The landlord had turned this space into an "office" primarily by removing all the kitchen appliances and the shower. So I dined mainly on toast and Campbell's soup and took my showers at my Grandma Mae's East Sacramento home. Grandma also wrote one of the paper's first columns, "Letter From Grandma." She worked cheap and never missed a deadline.

My first editorial for the biweekly *Suttertown Good-Time News* was written at dawn on my old boyhood desk, the only piece of furniture in the office other than the Murphy bed. In that first piece I lambasted a proposal to put a 12-story hotel across the street from the office, charging that another large concrete box would only "contribute to the decay" of downtown.

There followed a series of bold editorials that I hoped would shake up some of the solid citizens of Sacramento, at the very least spurring them to pick up the paper on a regular basis. I called for a complete ban of the automobile—"a filthy, foul-smelling public nuisance"—from downtown Sacramento. I wrote a millenium-is-coming editorial that predicted the complete collapse of the national economy and urged its replacement with a local economy based on handmade goods and community gardens.

The little paper boasted two employees: myself as publisher, editor, reporter, layout person and distribution agent; and a business manager named Michael Cunningham, a friend who had been hired on the basis of the meticulous mileage records he kept in the glove compartment of his BMW. Michael worked half time at the paper and wisely held on to his other part-time job as a lunchtime busboy in the restaurant downstairs.

As those early issues hit the streets we waited for the angry letters, phone calls, picket signs, whatever . . . but all was quiet. The phone rang once or twice during a typical business day. The couple in the apartment next door had more visitors than my crusading newspaper, and they were gone most of the day at teaching jobs. Very few subscribers were added to our charter list of 20, which consisted mostly of friends and relatives.

It wouldn't be long before I would be forced to sell my car to pay the newspaper's bills, reduced to putt-putting around town on a moped to collect past-due advertising dollars from shop owners as inexperienced as myself in business matters. As the *Suttertown Good-Time News'* art director and layout person, I learned as I went along. Since both advertising and articles were scarce, I filled last-minute gaping holes with drawings from old graphics books: pictures of farm animals, Gibson girls, anything I could find. In one issue I used a very large drawing of a cow to fill up half a page.

Because of our low circulation (never more than 1000 that first year) and bizarre graphics, *Suttertown* was not a publication that inspired confidence among potential advertisers. One after another, a series of initially optimistic ad salespeople would go forth singing the praises of the *Suttertown Good-Time News* to a skeptical business community. Some ad reps we never heard from again; few lasted more than a month.

One young man, a fundamentalist Christian with enormous optimism and incredible tenacity, managed to sell a series of big ads to a local supermarket by camping in the owner's office until a contract was signed. When the first sizeable check from that contract arrived in the mail, I thought, quite incorrectly as it turned out, that the paper's future was assured. But at least we had established ourselves as a publication very different from anything Sacramento had ever seen before.

There was some solid editorial stuff in the midst of those weird graphics. We hammered at the proposal for that 12-story hotel on the edge of what is now called midtown until the temperamental Reno developer promoting it gave up. I have to admit, though, that financial problems and the developer's tactless handling of the City Council did as much to kill the project as any editorial heat it got from *Suttertown*.

Around 1976, a small group of transit advocates proposed a light rail starter line that would run between CSUS and downtown. With the sole exception of one lone city councilman, the idea was greeted either with indifference or public guffaws from the mayor on down. The mayor, indeed, ridiculed it as a "Toonerville Trolley." *Suttertown*, in a page-one "Open Letter To The Mayor," asked what sort of alternative to traffic-clogged streets he proposed instead. This editorializing helped nudge the city toward support of an expanded starter line, essentially the system that we have today.

Affairs at the paper soon settled down to a slow, steady, week-by-week push to gain more subscribers, more outlets, more advertisers. You just took a deep breath on Monday and began the routine of nagging writers to meet deadlines, scrambling to pay the print bill and coping with aging, balky equipment.

The annual Christmas parties provided a welcome relief. Invitations went out with subscribers' papers. The subscribers and their friends and their friends' friends showed up in droves, packing our small second-floor office to the point where sometimes people were lined up outside on the stairway. If my fiery editorials didn't arouse the citizenry from their apathy, at least the parties did.

At one, a genuine fire-eater and sword-swallower who happened to be passing through town entertained the crowd. At another, a man who lived down the street and who claimed to be a descendant of European royalty, calling himself the "Count de Sessy," played classical pieces on the violin. Whether or not he was a real blueblood, he sure played a mean violin.

Yet another colorful party guest was Robert Simpson, the frail 90-year-old-man who roamed the state capitol's hallways every day in his walker, to which he had strapped picket signs denouncing then-governor Jerry Brown as a fraud and a liar. "It's hell being an idealist," he'd say as he pushed the walker along. His persistent political agitating was what kept him going, and as he beamed on the crowd that night I felt our feisty little paper had received his implicit blessing.

Despite the hardships, I feel more than a twinge of nostalgia for those early years that I spent waiting for the phone to ring in that dusty office. To my idealistic eyes, downtown Sacramento was a blank canvas waiting to be filled in with bold strokes from my editorial pen, aided by the efforts of our political allies. Yes, it was silly and naive of me to think that Sacramento would opt for a carless downtown or that shops with locally produced, handmade items would come to dominate the local economy. But it was the sense of creative possibility behind those ideas that was important.

Now much of the canvas is covered, and so far it resembles the work of an unimaginative weekend painter. Granted, we have public art, light rail and that other radical innovation, sidewalk seating. But the basic direction of downtown Sacramento hasn't changed much in the last 30 years. We're still trying to mimic big-city skylines, and we still believe that the only real hope for downtown's commercial sector is to attract hordes of shoppers from the suburbs. Meanwhile, downtown neighborhoods continue to be inundated with the increasingly heavy traffic that is the direct result of these policies.*

So here I am at 45, newspaperless, a little belatedly looking for a decent-paying job. I'll always be grateful for the opportunity I've had to pursue a personal dream for nearly two decades. I guess it was inevitable that some day I'd have to wake up.

*A ray of hope occurred shortly after this article appeared in a 1994 issue of The Sacramento Bee, in the form of a "traffic-calming" plan for the northeast quadrant of midtown Sacramento. Surprisingly, car-obsessed Sacramento opted to experiment with devices such as half-street closures and traffic circles designed to slow cars down. Even more surprisingly, the experiment seems to be successful.

SMALL TOWN
LIFE

AS COMFORTABLE AS AN OLD SHOE

I live in a long, boxcar-shaped town, nestled in the cool, green canyon carved by the Sacramento River. Dunsmuir is small in population (1923 souls, by last count), but rich in natural resources. It has clean air, clean water, thick forests on all sides, and the majestic presence of Mount Shasta looming up on the northern horizon.

But for me one of its chief attractions is that it's a place where old shoes will do just as well as new ones, where comfortable old clothes will do just as well as new ones on the town's streets.

It is a working-class town, an old railroad town. The railroad has reduced its workforce over the years, but Dunsmuir still is home to a lot of retired railroad workers, who tend to set the standard in fashion—for men, anyway. For most of us that means flannel shirts or t-shirts and bluejeans. And if these are well-worn and even a bit tattered at times, no one will particularly notice. There's something healthy about this; it allows room for all the bulges and wrinkles and quirks that would otherwise get smoothed out under the latest fashions.

A ruddy-faced, middle-aged guy showed up at the hardware store the other day looking about as pleased with himself as anyone could be. On the front of his old down vest he prominently displayed, over a tear in the fabric, a four-inch strip of duct tape. This is a man with a solid sense of self-worth, I would say, who by his makeshift clothing says to his fellow citizens, "Take me as I am; I have no need to impress you"—although, for all Dunsmuir cared, that duct tape could just as well have been a silk handkerchief.

Dunsmuir is a town where retired hoboes and retired librarians mingle on the main street. Carolyn, the Town Bookworm, parades up and down the main street the livelong day, swaying from side to side on her spindly legs as she peruses her latest find from the library (an urban planning study of Rio de Janiero on our last encounter—she has to dig pretty deep nowadays to find anything she hasn't read).

Don Desimone, a retired hobo whose moniker was "Roadhog," wears a Santa Claus costume and passes out candy canes on the main street at Christmastime. It is something of a role reversal for a man who likes to boast that in his hobo days, soliciting handouts and odd jobs, he "got turned down more times than a bedsheet."

Dunsmuir is in something of a backwater. In earlier times, the interstate freeway ran right through the middle of town, but now it soars above and around us, and because of that and the decline of the railroad we do not have the hustle and bustle on the streets that we had in those bygone days. This gives our town characters more elbow room, more of a chance to stand out and at the same time work themselves into the social fabric of the community.

A very different town lies only a few miles to the north of us, in the shadow of majestic Mount Shasta.

This neighboring town is, compared to our humble town, an exotic and enchanting place, a town where carpenters have the faces of poets, where burgundy-robed monks shop in the local grocery store.

The array of personalities one encounters there is at once stimulating, dazzling, and a little overwhelming. It is a town much of whose population seems to be auditioning for a multitude of self-created roles. There is a level of striving, of yearning for something undefined, that tends to put me on edge. It is New York mellowed by New Age consciousness. At any rate, I am glad after my little shopping sprees to return to my little railroad town.

Here in Dunsmuir the auditions, if there ever were any, were completed long before I arrived. If our more colorful denizens are playing roles, they've been doing it so long that the line between self and adopted self is seamless. They wear their identities, borrowed or otherwise, just as easily as you would an old pair of shoes.

SMALL TOWN SMALL TALK

*T*hose of you who are glib of tongue, with an apt remark always at the ready, can't truly understand the agonies of the conversationally challenged. We are thankful you exist, because while you are spinning out your effortless stream of verbiage, we're straining to think of something, anything to say. (And by the time we do the conversation, or monologue, has moved on to other topics.) The Sahara Desert is a veritable Garden of Eden compared with the vast, empty stretches of our conversational landscape.

But for me, things have been looking up recently, conversation-wise. I moved from the big city of Sacramento to a small town in Northern California, and I have been picking up lessons and encouragement in the art of small talk.

When I moved here, I promised myself I would adapt as best I could to small-town life. I would slow down and take time to actually *talk* to people. In the city one seems to have very little time to chat. There is so much to do, so many things to accomplish. In my previous life as the publisher and editor and all-around-go-fer of a weekly newspaper, people often seemed to be annoying impediments to getting the paper out every week. I mean, they often wanted to talk to me for no apparent reason, just to *visit*, for goodness sake.

In a small town, visiting is central, not peripheral, to life. When you walk out of your house and encounter someone you know, which of course will occur on every block, you are naturally expected to stop and exchange a few words. The same is true when you go into a shop or the post office or the grocery store. A simple comment on the weather to the clerk behind the counter will not suffice. You *know* this person, after all, so your remarks should not be generic, but customized.

This leads me to the big advantage the small-town small talker has, especially those of us at the training-wheel stage. My mind may be a blank, but the fact that I *know* the other person means I can ask all sorts of questions about his or her spouse, kids, girl-friend/boyfriend, job, whatever. Start observing skilled small-talkers, and you'll find this is a common technique.

In the city, the classic small-talk situation is the 10-to-15-second ride in the elevator. You are thrown together with another person, and the alternative to an awkward silence is to exchange three or four sentences. So you take the plunge: You have to avoid false starts and be prepared to carry on a short monologue in case your fellow traveler is unresponsive. The standard pattern here is an opening line, then a response from the other person (sometimes) and a closing remark (ideally in the form of a succinct, witty remark) delivered over your shoulder as you exit.

Is this small talk? Well, maybe, but it bears about the same relation to real small talk that instant decaf bears to real coffee. Big-city time-crunch pressure distorts the whole interaction. As a result, you experience the kind of pressure stand-up comics feel on opening night, except at least they get another try if their first line bombs.

In the typical small-town encounter, seconds stretch to minutes. If there's a false start, a conversational ploy that leads nowhere, there's plenty of time to try another tack, and your experienced small-towner will be happy to jump in with the needed fresh topic.

In the fast-paced, big-city encounter, the pressure is on to dazzle and entertain. In the small-town version, there is time to listen and exchange information. The range of topics is broadened, because some topics, particularly those touching on human relationships, can't be skimmed over. And since you are much more likely to know each other, you have a wealth of topics not available to strangers.

But there is still a major hurdle: the conversation closer. Have you ever found yourself in a lively and interesting conversation that slowly slides toward the mundane and boring because neither of you can figure out how to end it?

This one is a challenge for every conscientious small talker, no matter where he or she lives, but the small-town folks I've encountered often deal with it by simply taking a more generous, accepting attitude than I usually encountered in the big city. There, if by considerable effort I summoned up a mildly witty remark as a closer, I would usually be greeted with a blank look or a "yeah, if you say so" kind of response. Worse, my remark might be misinterpreted as an introduction to a whole new line of conversation.

Here that same remark might cause my listener's face to brighten up a bit. A chuckle or two might slip out. I know from experience that my comment doesn't really merit that kind of response; the smile and the chuckle are really meant to convey this underlying message: I'm glad I ran into you, I value and respect you as a fellow human being, and I enjoy sharing a little time with you once in a while.

That message is the essence of good small talk. Like all the other gifts we give each other, it's not what's actually said or done that's important, but the thought behind it.

SERENDIPITY ON THE TRAILS

*W*hen I first started visiting the little Northern California town of Dunsmuir in the mid-1980s, it was mainly a roots thing. A friend of mine who knew I liked small towns suggested I go there since it was indeed small (pop. 1923) and my parents grew up there.

I was leading a frazzled life in those days, and a sojourn in a quiet, isolated mountain town seemed like just the thing. And since my dad had died when I was 5 and my mother when I was 18, there were a lot of gaps in my immediate family's history that might be filled on such a trip.

My first view of Dunsmuir was at 10 o'clock on a crisp December evening. The Greyhound had dropped me off in front of one of the town's two bars. As I got off the bus I felt as if I had stepped back 40 years. Architecturally, no apparent changes had been made on that main street since the 1940s, right down to the ornate town clock in front of the Timberline Community Bank.

Once in town, I wasted little time setting out on my roots journey. Early success (or so I thought) came in the form of a sweet-voiced elderly lady who, when I mentioned my mother's name on the phone, exclaimed, "Lodemia Quigley?! Why, I walked to school with her every day!"

This article was written during the winter of 1995/1996.

Naturally, I was eager to sit down and talk with this lady, a potential treasure trove of memories about my mother's early years. But I had called her just before Christmas, and relatives were literally streaming through her front door as we spoke. We agreed to meet the next time I visited Dunsmuir.

"Lodemia Quigley . . . well, let's see, what can I tell you? . . ." she said, somewhat hesitantly, as we sat at her kitchen table the following spring. "You know, what I remember about her was that she was . . . she was . . . well, she was just *real clean.*" She repeated that phrase several times.

Unfortunately, this proved to be the sum total of her memories of my mother. After 50 years, those memories were dim if reassuringly hygienic. This particular roots trail had, after a promising start, ended abruptly. But there would be other trails to follow.

As time wore on and my visits grew more frequent, I became more and more enchanted with the little town and its alpine surroundings. Last year I set up housekeeping there in a small, brightly painted home with full-window views of the thickly forested hills. I love to hike and was soon out exploring, sometimes following trails and sometimes, with a foolhardy pioneer spirit, making my own trails.

It was shortly after moving there that I found myself following a narrow deer trail along one hillside. Suddenly the trail plunged into someone's blooming hillside garden, strewn with flowers and a wealth of green vegetables. In a strange mixture of the wild and tame, I encountered bear droppings in the middle of the garden's path—a delightfully serendipitous ending to this deadend trail.

Rounding a turn in front of the garden-owner's house, I encountered the man himself, a crusty old gent who started sputtering phrases about property rights and intruders, but who mellowed considerably when I told him about the family roots journey that had originally brought me to this place.

"Your mother may have been born on this very spot," he solemnly informed me. He explained that the town hospital had once occupied the same patch of ground as his garden. He and his wife lived in the house formerly inhabited by the hospital's doctor.

This roots "discovery" turned out to be another false trail. I recently learned after checking my mother's death certificate in Sacramento that, while she certainly grew up in Dunsmuir, she was born in Bakersfield.

On another hiking expedition near Dunsmuir, I reached a high ridge top by following a well-marked trail. When I got to the top of the ridge, the view was breathtaking. There was a whole sea of mountains spread out before me, wave after wave of mountain ridges fading into the blue horizon. It was a spectacular visual reward for a few hours of hiking, and certainly no deadend trail.

But deadend trails have their own kind of value. You never know what sort of unexpected gardens you'll find along the way.

More Quality Paperbacks
From Suttertown Publishing

On Higher Ground • A Postmodern Romance

On Higher Ground, by Tim Holt, is a sometimes hopeful, sometimes ominous portrayal of Northern California in the mid-21st century. This futuristic novel chronicles the struggles and human dramas of the Mount Shasta region, where a new society is emerging above the domed cities and scorched earth of the valley below. 280 pgs. $12.95.

The Pilgrims' Chorus • A Coming-Of-Age Story

In *The Pilgrims' Chorus*, a coming-of-age novel about a young dog who joins a wolf pack, you'll find the kind of enchanting characters that fill the pages of *Wind In The Willows*.

There's Barnabus, a wise old dog and the keeper of the book's great secret. And Dream Talker, the charming misfit of the wolf pack—a philosopher-wolf who speaks of his beloved woods and wilderness in the language of poetry.

A book for adults young and old who love a good story well told. 124 pgs. $7.95.

Old River Town • A Personal History Of Sacramento

In *Old River Town*, Lloyd Bruno, who came to Sacramento in 1923, revels in the romance of its steamboats, its trolleys, and its vaguely Southern charm.

In this beautifully written, very personal history, readers will learn of such long-forgotten but important Sacramento institutions as the McNeill Club and the X Club from someone who was an active participant in both. They will also learn more about some of Sacramento's colorful personalities, including John Sutter, C.K. McClatchy and Belle Cooledge. 124 pgs. $13.95

Check Your Local Independent Bookstore For These Titles, Or Order Direct From The Publisher

Add $2.25 for shipping and tax for single book orders, $1.25 shipping and tax for each additional book ordered. No cash, please. Make check or money order payable to "Tim Holt," P.O. Box 214, Dunsmuir, California 96025. Phone number: (530) 235-4034.